D1071590

Cheryl Payer's Previous Books

The Debt Trap: The IMF and the Third World (London: Penguin, 1974, and New York: Monthly Review, 1975)

"This excellent book deserves a warm welcome from all engaged in the study of political economy as a model of its kind. It is readable enough, too, to appeal to a wide public."
Malcolm Caldwell: *Journal of Contemporary Asia.*

"Highly recommended. . . . A valuable resource for the student of the international capitalist system."
Martin Landsberg: *Insurgent Sociologist.*

"A pioneering study."
Walden Bello: *Development Debacle.*

"An easy-to-read, insightful analysis. . . . An excellent introduction to international finance."
Lenny Siegel: *Pacific Research and World Empire Telegram.*

The World Bank: A Critical Analysis (New York: Monthly Review Press, 1982)

"The long-awaited companion volume to the author's widely acclaimed *The Debt Trap* . . . well written and well researched. . . . Essential for most libraries."
Ronnie J. Phillips: *Library Journal.*

"An important and provocative interpretation of the political economy of a powerful international organization."
John Ikenberry: *American Political Science Review.*

"Not only a scholarly analysis of the Bank, but also new insights into the constraints on development in the Third World."
Harry Magdoff: Co-editor, *Monthly Review.*

"By far the most outstanding work in the literature about the Bank."
Ernest Feder: *Economic and Political Weekly.*

Lent and Lost

Foreign Credit and Third World Development

Cheryl Payer

Zed Books Ltd
London and New Jersey

Lent and Lost was first published by Zed Books Ltd,
57 Caledonian Road, London N1 9BU, UK, and 165 First Avenue,
Atlantic Highlands, New Jersey 07716, USA, in 1991.

Cover designed by Sophie Buchet.
Typeset by EMS Photosetters, Thorpe Bay, Essex.
Printed and bound in the United Kingdom
by Biddles Ltd, Guildford and King's Lynn.

British Library Cataloguing in Publication Data

Payer, Cheryl, 1940
Lent and lost : foreign credit and Third World development.
1. Developing countries : Economic conditions : Financial assistance
I. Title
338.91091724

ISBN 0-86232-952-3
ISBN 0-86232-953-1 pbk

Contents

Tables and Graphs

Acknowledgements

In twenty years of writing on Third World debt, the author has drawn upon the experience and generosity of too many people and institutions to be recalled here. To try to name some of them would inevitably mean to slight others unfairly.

I must, however, thank a handful of economists who have carefully read and given me comments on earlier drafts of this book. They are Penny Ciancanelli, Polly Allen, James Boyce, Dragoslav Avramović, Ole David Koht Norbye and Keith Griffin. They do not necessarily agree with my conclusions and are not responsible for my errors.

I am grateful for the support of the Christian Michelsen Institute in Bergen, Norway, which made it possible for me to spend a total of six months enjoying their excellent library and the company of their scholars. Thanks to Jan Isaksen, Acting Director of the CMI when the grant was made, for his confidence in this project.

Finally, I must acknowledge the contribution of the audiences at the many colleges, universities, community groups and conferences where I have been invited to lecture over the past twenty years. Their questions, comments and objections have forced me to sharpen, discard and/or reexamine many arguments. They have also affirmed me in my belief in the importance of the topic of this book.

Introduction

Since the Latin American debt crisis broke in 1982, Third World debtors have been paying their creditors an average of $30 billion more each year than they have received in new lending. This is money which could and should be used to pay for necessary imports to keep their own productive facilities operating and to make new investments for future production. It is money that is desperately needed for education and health care expenditures. It is money that has to be squeezed out of those taxpayers who cannot avoid being taxed in taxation systems which are grossly unfair and allow the richest to escape their fair share of taxes. It is a charge that they are legally required to pay year after year, into the indefinite future.

Although the average citizen of the United States or Europe may not be aware of this enormous drain of capital from the parts of the world they think of as being pitifully poor, the 'experts' on the debt crisis are well aware of it. Some, like the banks which collect most of the money as interest on past debts, tell us that this is necessary so that the debtor countries can regain access to international capital markets, which would be closed to them if they repudiated or otherwise failed to pay. Some, like US Senator Bill Bradley, advocate that payments be reduced for some countries because the debtors cannot pay for exports of goods and services from the United States when they have to pay such huge tribute to the banks. And some, mainly opposition groups in the debtor countries themselves, advocate repudiation of the debt or a moratorium on interest payments which would – in the eyes of creditors – be tantamount to repudiation.

This is not a book about the devastating human costs and consequences of Third World debt, although concern for those costs underlies all the author's work on the subject. There are other excellent works on that topic.[1] Nor does this attempt a comprehensive history of the crisis.

Why, then, is another book on the debt crisis needed? Because almost all of the participants in the debate about Third World debt share the same misconceptions about Third World development and the role of foreign capital in that development that led directly to the debt crisis. Most of the prescriptions offered for the 'solution' of this crisis will fail because they do not understand that their premises are false. Unless we correct some of the dangerous myths which led us into the present mess, we cannot solve the present crisis; even less can we prevent the same thing happening in the future.

Some of the myths which this book will demolish are:

- Myth: Poor countries are natural importers of capital. (Fact: In the 1980s they have been massive exporters of capital, and even when they were importers there was nothing natural about the process.)
- Myth: The debt crisis was caused by the OPEC price hikes of the 1970s, which forced oil importers into debt. (Fact: The debt crisis was around long before the oil price rises, and many oil exporters are deeper in debt than the oil importers.)
- Myth: The International Monetary Fund and the World Bank know how to advise countries to correct balance of payments problems. (Fact: The IMF and the World Bank have themselves been major causes of the debt crises of their Third World clients, and have not changed their advice even after the crisis broke.)
- Myth: Debtor countries are in trouble because they borrowed for consumption, rather than investment. (Fact: The conditions for successful use of foreign capital are much more stringent than this facile formula suggests, and very few critics who now enjoy twenty-twenty hindsight were suggesting this when the expenditures were made.)
- Myth: Third World debtors will never get any new foreign capital unless they are scrupulous about meeting their old obligations. (Fact: They will not get any new capital unless their old obligations are extinguished through repudiation or forgiveness.)
- Myth: Economic growth will give citizens of the debtor countries a better life, while at the same time eventually allowing them to pay off their debts. (Fact: Domestic growth worsens balance-of-payments problems rather than solving them.)

The debt crisis has been a long time in the making: since the end of World War II, in fact. It has been the inevitable result of a fundamental contradiction in US economic policy toward the so-called developing countries. And the deepest irony of the contradiction is that the enormous and outrageous drain of badly needed capital from these presumably poor countries has been the direct result of the ideology of development which insists that these poor countries require *large and sustained inflows* of foreign capital for their development.

The most decent humanitarian impulses of the US and European people have been exploited in support of 'foreign aid' programs which have led directly, as the following book will show, to the extraction of wealth from these countries. In the process millions of inhabitants of these debtor countries who were not really so poor – in the sense of lacking basic human needs – have been genuinely impoverished. Their land has been expropriated for agribusiness enterprises. Their labour unions have been outlawed. Their small factories and handicrafts have been driven out of business by cheap imports (financed by foreign aid). Their government officials have been corrupted by the huge amounts of money flowing through their hands as aid or development loans.

The crowning irony is that the creditors are now taking money out of these countries because a few years ago they lent it to them. There is nothing surprising about this; indeed, it is so banal it is hardly worth mentioning. That is the way loans are supposed to operate. What is surprising is that few people thought about this problem when the money was flowing in, and those who did warn of it were ignored, ridiculed and refuted. It was too lucrative and convenient for too many people, both in government and in the private banks, to ignore the warning signals. But the ordinary people in the debtor countries, who benefited little if at all from the borrowed money, are now suffering the disaster of servicing the debt.

This book strikes at the jugular of conventional development theory: the belief that a constant flow of large amounts of foreign capital is a necessary – even a sufficient – condition for the success of the ill-defined process called 'economic development'. It shows how the creditor nations' use of these capital flows for their own political and economic goals led inevitably to a global debt crisis. And it suggests that in future such international flows of funds must be subjected to stringent controls of a strictly non-political nature if the disaster of the 1980s is not to be repeated.

A word must be said about the scope of this book. Because it focuses on the self-interest and self-delusions associated with loan capital, it is not specifically a critique of private foreign investment or of governmental or private grant aid. It should not, however, be read as an endorsement of these alternative forms of funds transfer; indeed, most of the caveats about ascribing any special qualities to 'foreign capital' apply equally to foreign investment and grant aid. Direct investment shares with foreign loans the candid objective of taking out of a country more than is brought in; while grants share with loans the detrimental effects of harmful conditionality, competition with local producers, and the encouragement of waste and corruption. In addition, grant aid is usually designed to induce long-term dependence on costly imports of specialized inputs or spare parts obtainable only from the donor.

The argument is meant to be applicable to all areas of the Third World. Parts of it will also be relevant to debtor countries in Eastern Europe, which it appears are now to be handed over to the clutches of the International Monetary Fund, and even to other developed countries, such as Australia and Canada, which are international debtors.[2] The largest foreign debt crisis of all, that of the United States, still lies in the future.

Although the theoretical argument aspires to universal application, every country situation is unique; this is not a definitive analysis of every debtor country on the face of the globe. Examples have been taken as needed, with no attempt to cover all areas. This may lead to the impression that this is a book about Latin American debt, because the problem has been more fully developed over the decades there than in Africa, where more debt is held by public than private creditors, or in Asia, where many country crises either lie in the future or have been 'bailed out' by the Japanese. But the central argument of the book abstracts from the differences among the continents, and the even more striking differences among countries on the same continent, to seek the essential relationships which have resulted in one single overriding crisis for many absurdly disparate countries.

On the creditor side, this book deals only with the policies of the United States government. This focus is justified because, over the period covered by this book the United States has played the dominant role both in amounts of aid and of private bank lending, and in its policy leadership among its capitalist allies. Great Britain and France both have aid programs focused mainly on their former colonies – an important clue to the function of aid.

The policies of these countries towards the Third World differ in details from that of the United States but not in essence, e.g. the heavy emphasis on promoting their own exports and businesses, including highly paid technical consultants tied-in with exporters of plant and machinery produced in that country. Even countries such as Canada and Norway, which pride themselves on progressive policies towards the Third World, are not exempt from this criticism.[3] Nor have these countries showed much independence or courage in refusing to fall into line with the other members of the creditors' cartel behind the policy conditionality of the IMF and the World Bank.

Since the early years of the presidency of Ronald Reagan the United States is, globally speaking, no longer a creditor nation but a debtor. This fact is closely connected with its loss of relative power and prestige among its capitalist allies. Since the interest of the US government is to prevent any major changes in their Third World policy, they hope to co-opt the huge foreign exchange reserves of Japan to the service of their old policies. In the language of this book, Japan would then become the next sucker in the Ponzi scheme, bailing out previous bad debts with a continued emphasis on IMF and World Bank conditionality.

However, there is good reason to believe that, by virtue of its foreign exchange resources, Japan has already become the dominant creditor nation in the Third World as a whole (as it has long been in Asia) and could overrule the United States on debt policy anytime it wished to take up that responsibility. Since we do not know in what ways Japan's policies will differ from the past policies of the United States in that respect, we can not say for certain that the arguments of this book can be transferred without modifications to predictions of future trends. If the argument is sound, however, this book will aid the reader to an understanding of the choices and limits faced by any dominant creditor and its debtors.

Part One: Concepts

In the first section of this volume, we introduce some concepts which are the basic building blocks of our argument. The reader of these short introductory chapters will then be able to follow the decade-by-decade history of the gestation of the debt crisis in the next section, and will be better equipped to judge the conclusions contained in the last part of the book.

First, we assert that there is a fundamental contradiction in US foreign policy towards the Third World: two goals – the perpetual one-way flow of money to the Third World, and the desire to make private enterprise the vehicle of these flows – which are over the long run mutually incompatible. The incompatibility between these two goals and their inevitable collision is the cause of the debt crisis.

The next chapter explains the 'net transfer', or the relationship between what comes into a country in new lending and what goes out in debt service, and why this is a more meaningful indicator of problems than the better-known 'debt service ratio'. In Chapter 3 we explain why the con game known as the Ponzi scheme is an apt metaphor for the postwar history of Third World debt.

The 'transfer problem' (which is not the same as the 'net transfer'), or the necessary relationship between international flows of money and international flows of goods and services, is discussed in Chapter 4. Chapter 5 discusses one influential article on the benefits of transferring funds and resources from rich (surplus) to poor (deficit) countries.

Two models constructed by economists for the purpose of justifying capital flows are criticised in Chapter 6. Finally, in Chapter 7 we consider the role of economic growth in making possible repayment of debt, and develop a critique of the widely held notion that every country passes through balance-of-payments stages, from debtor to creditor, in the course of development.

1. The contradictions of capital transfer

Everyone who uses a credit card knows that you cannot spend more than you earn for a prolonged period of time without getting into trouble. And yet the conventional wisdom of development economics has been that this is exactly what Third World nations should do, because they are poor.

Everyone who has borrowed money knows that at some point, usually not too far into the future, the borrower has to pay more to his creditor than he has received from the creditor, and that over the life of the loan this excess is *much* higher than the amount that was originally borrowed.

And yet it has long been considered 'natural' for capital to flow in one direction only from the developed industrial economies to the Third World. A splendid illustration of this mentality is found in the first chapter of an otherwise very good book on the debt crisis:

> Until 1982 it was understood that there had to be, for a prolonged period, a one-way flow of resources from the advanced countries to the Third World to promote its development. The view went unchallenged in either official or private-sector circles and was supported by every school of thought, albeit for different reasons. Since the debt crisis which broke in 1982, these flows have been reversed for each important group of countries in the Third World . . .
>
> *This reverse or negative flow is a perversion of common sense, and of sound economics.* On a classical view, the developing countries should attract capital from the industrial world because they are able to increase output by more than rich countries for a given increase in investment. On an alternative view, the debtors need balance-of-payment finance because their domestic economies are capable of expanding more rapidly than they are able to increase their foreign exchange earnings and imports . . . To our knowledge, no economist has yet advocated a large flow of resources from the poorer countries as a way of stimulating their economic progress.
>
> *Nor was this ever the intention of those who encouraged or undertook the original lending to the debtors*, the interest payments on which are the main cause of the reverse transfer. *It was always implicitly assumed* that the financial markets would continue to refinance old debt and extend new credit so that the flow of resources to the developing world would continue,

> at least until some *far-distant future* in which the debtors would reach a level of development where it was feasible and desirable for them to export rather than import capital.[4]

Other authorities agree. The Organisation for Economic Cooperation and Development (OECD), summarising twenty-five years of international capital flows, describes

> what was generally regarded as a *logical and healthy* process in which savings flowed from capital-rich to capital-poor countries . . . The broad picture . . . [was] a current account (savings) surplus in industrial countries of around 0.7–1.0 per cent of their combined GNPs and a current account (savings) deficit in developing countries, taken together, in the region of 2.0–2.5 per cent of their combined GNPs.[5]

In practice, there was nothing at all 'natural' about the flows of capital from the industrial countries to the Third World. The natural impulse of banks and other creditors in the decades following the defaults of Latin American borrowers in the 1930s was to *avoid* lending to that part of the world. They preferred to do business within their own countries and with other wealthy countries.

> Even ordinary exports in the postwar period would not be financed by exporters and their banks without government guarantees . . . There are probably few credits, except some bank credits, which in some way or another are not financially assisted by the governments of the industrial countries, *if only to the extent of assuming the risk of nonpayment*.[6]

Even worse for the theory, those Latin Americans who did have capital preferred to hold it in bank accounts or other investments in Europe or New York. Latin America was a major *source* of Eurodollar deposits as long ago as the 1960s!

> The market has always been full of stories about the courier leaving Rio for Geneva every Friday afternoon with hundreds of thousands of dollars in cash.[7]

'Indeed', one Latin American specialist wrote in 1971, 'the problem is not to attract foreign savings but to prevent the region's savings from leaking abroad . . . [The Economic Commission for Latin America's] estimate of the total net outflow of private domestic capital from Latin America is $5,000 million over the period 1946–62.'[8]

Just as flows of capital from rich countries to poor (or from North to South) were considered 'natural', so the reversal of these flows – capital flowing *out* of poor countries to service debts – is widely considered to be 'abnormal', 'perverse' and 'bad economics' by most of those who comment on it.

Yet, from the point of view of the commercial loan contract, this relationship is not perverse at all, but the natural, intended and inevitable consequence of a loan. *Every loan goes through this cycle, unless it is defaulted or forgiven.* The only exceptions are so-called 'loans' which are made on such soft terms that they are virtually a grant.

The loan cycle

If we study the 'life cycle' of one loan only, this is easy to see. In 1972, Charles R. Frank, Jr., charted the life cycle of a loan on what were then World Bank terms of twenty-five years' maturity, five-year grace periods, and 7 per cent interest (see graph 1).[9]

In this graph, the solid line with the lower 'hump' indicates the flow of funds to the borrower. The line with the higher, 'peaked' hump indicates the flow of funds which the *borrower* will have to pay as interest and amortisation. The line which lies mainly *below* the base line charts the difference between the gross capital flow and the debt service, or what is called the 'net transfer'. This concept will be explained further in the following chapter. Note that the transfer is positive, that is, the borrowers receive more money than they pay out, only for the first twenty years of the cycle of more than eighty years. Note also the enormous depth of the line for a thirty-year period (between years 40 and 70) during which the debt service payments far exceed the total amount received.

If we now consider that in the real world we are about 'year 30' on this graph, it will be clear how far we are from restoring net capital flows from North to South *through normal market mechanisms*.

Even if we used other assumptions in constructing the model, for example that loans are extended on very 'soft' terms, with low interest rates and long maturities, we would have a profile with a flatter hump and a longer life but the basic relationship would not be changed: *capital flows in the form of loans must inevitably reverse themselves at some point.*

In short, the cause of the debt crisis was an inbuilt contradiction between a macroeconomic theory that holds it natural for Third World countries to import capital for long periods of time, and the microeconomic marketplace (or quasi-marketplace) instruments (commercial and government-subsidised loans) through which this transfer was accomplished.

In theory, flows of capital to the Third World are supposed to be invested in productive enterprises which will eventually produce an export surplus from which they can easily service their foreign debts. There are two problems with this scenario. The first, which will be investigated at greater length in the penultimate chapter, is that for most debtor countries it did not happen that way. The second is that if the theory had worked as predicted, the consequences for the *creditor* countries, in terms of loss of markets and competition at home, would have been catastrophic for their own economies.

What went wrong? The fault does not lie in the loan contract. If private

Figure 1.1
Capital inflows and outflows on a loan at near-market interest rates

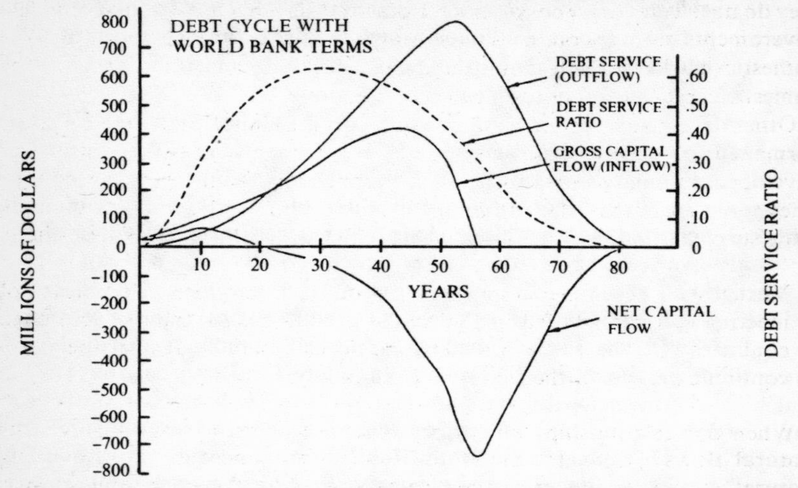

Source: Charles R. Frank, Jr., "Debt and Terms of Aid," in Overseas Development Council, *Assisting Developing Countries* (Praeger, 1972) p. 31.

lenders give up the use of their money they require a recompense. That is a law of economic behaviour, which cannot be repealed any more than can the law of gravity. (Governments are not subject to the same rules, a fact which we shall return to later.)

This does not mean, of course, that the lenders were not at fault. Of course they bear a heavy share of responsibility for the *débâcle* of Third World debt, and should be made to pay a heavy share of the cost. But their behaviour must be understood within its policy context.

The fault lies primarily with US policy makers (followed and copied uncritically by the leaders of other major Western nations), who encouraged chronic borrowing on the part of Third World countries, encouraged economists to create the theoretical justification for this borrowing and eventually succeeded in getting private enterprise – the commercial banks – to bail out their own stalled lending operations. In so doing they succeeded merely in postponing the crisis of Third World debt for one or two decades. The world is paying now for that temporary postponement.

The US government had two fundamental reasons for encouraging Third World states to depend on foreign borrowing, one economic and one political.

The developed market economies, led by the United States, have become dependent on running an export surplus to the Third World. Some countries, notably Japan and Germany, have economies which have become structurally dependent on running trade surpluses with the rest of the world.

These countries have strong business classes, who gain a double advantage from these trade surpluses: they gain markets for their products overseas, and they do not suffer heavy competition from imports in their home markets. The governments of these countries resist pressures to allow more imports into the domestic market, which would balance their trade accounts, because the domestic capitalists do not want the competition.

Other developed Western economies such as the United States do not enjoy permanent or structural surpluses. They are frequently in deficit with other developed trading partners and even in overall deficit on their trade accounts. They, even more than the structural surplus countries, depend on running a trade surplus with the Third World because this helps offset deficits elsewhere.

> Virtually all developed countries insist on trade surpluses. One means of meeting this strongly felt imperative of the 1970s is for the less developed countries (LDCs) to be provided the development finance to permit a continuing excess of their imports over exports.[10]

When this relationship, which they consider almost a natural order (the 'natural' flows of capital to the Third World have financed the corresponding 'natural' export surplus of the creditors) is reversed, the US becomes nasty. Witness its current behaviour towards Taiwan, South Korea and Brazil, who have recently enjoyed trade surpluses with the United States. Although these are the so-called success stories of Third World development, their export surpluses are met with retaliation, constant threats to erect more trade barriers and heavy-handed pressure to open up their own internal markets.

Taiwan's surplus was achieved without a heavy debt build-up; South Korea and Brazil must achieve a strong export surplus and maintain it for many years if they are to be able to service their debts. Most other Third World debtors have achieved an export surplus only because their imports were sharply curtailed in the wake of the debt crisis. Although the latter have been fulsomely praised for this 'achievement', the fact is that they had no choice: the financing which had in previous years supported their import surpluses had dried up. You can't import if you can't get credit and don't have cash to pay.

This was a painful operation for most of these countries, Brazil included. In contrast to the North, where strong business elites had persuaded the government to finance their export surpluses to the Third World, business classes in the South were relatively weak. Their need for markets had often been ignored by governments tempted by the opportunity to consume more than the nation produced and to spend more than the government could collect in taxes. And, as the interests of productive businesses were ignored, other business interests grew up which were dependent on the distribution and sale of *imported* goods, and on the corruption and kickbacks which usually accompanied this.[11]

Thus, as the North became structurally dependent on exporting more to the Third World than it imported, the South developed a social structure addicted to the complementary distortion of a chronic import surplus. And, since the South was spending more on imports (and other necessary payments such as profit remittance to foreign investors) than it earned in exports, it was necessary to balance the accounts by grants or loans from the exporting countries.

But there was also a compelling political reason for the flow of resources to Third World countries. Foreign aid and the import of capital have been used by the United States and other industrial nations as a bribe with which to purchase compliant behaviour. In its crudest form, the behaviour which creditors wished to influence could be the purchase of votes at the UN or other international forums; it could be an agreement to prevent communist or other radical parties from participating in a government. Indeed, such tactics have even been used against the United States' more developed allies.[12]

In its most sophisticated form, credits have been used to persuade governments to accept complex economic programs designed by the International Monetary Fund and the World Bank. The object of the economic programs prescribed by these institutions is precisely the opposite of what it pretends to be. Whereas the pretence is that the conditions will enable the borrowing country to achieve a healthier balance of trade and payments, the real purpose, and the effect, of the programs is to bribe the governments to *prevent* them from making the economic changes which would make them more independent and self-supporting.[13]

On the whole, this use of foreign aid and other capital flows as a bribe has been one of the most successful and effective tools of foreign economic policy. Only in cases where bribery fails does the US government find it necessary to employ military force or threats (Nicaragua, Grenada, Libya and Panama are obvious recent examples).

When money flows from South to North, therefore, this is a crisis for the North as well as for the South – *even, and especially, if the borrower is able to service the debt*. This negative flow means that the United States and other industrialised countries lose export markets and see their home markets invaded by Third World products to an unprecedented extent. It also means that the United States loses one of its most powerful tools for controlling the behaviour of the debtor governments.

There is a fundamental, unavoidable, inbuilt contradiction between the two basic tenets of US economic policy towards the Third World. It is a system built to self-destruct! These two tenets are as follows:

1. The desire to run a perpetually unbalanced trade (a perennial export surplus) with the Third World. This unbalanced trade has to be financed by an unbalanced capital flow to those Third World governments which the creditor nations want to support and/or control.

2. The belief that this capital flow to the Third World can be carried out by private capital, whether in the form of direct investment or loans, and by official loans at near-market terms, such as those of the World Bank or the Eximbank.

The contradiction is this: private businesses and banks expect to earn interest on their loans and profit on their investments. They expect *either* eventual repayment or interest payments in perpetuity in the case of loans, and they suffer losses if they do not receive such payments. But, as the money is repaid (or interest mounts) the 'natural' flow of capital from North to South is *necessarily* reversed.

If the money is repaid, the creditor countries must accept import surpluses in a magnitude sufficient to match the flow of funds, thus a negative trade balance with the same debtors with whom they have previously enjoyed export surpluses. This creates difficulties for exporters and workers in the creditor countries, who lose customers and acquire cutthroat competitors. It also means that the interest of exporters (at least those who are not multinational, with an ability to shift their production base to other countries), labour and the economy as a whole is in direct conflict with the interest of the banks. 'Although it is widely recognised that US banks face the prospect of collapse if debtors did not pay, it is less well understood that US workers and businesses lose jobs and markets as the Latin Americans try to pay.'[14]

And, if the money is not repaid, the big question must be, who will bear the cost of nonpayment? Will it be the businesses which made the investment or the loan? In that case, other businesses may be hesitant to make a similar loan or investment in the (near) future.

Or is it to be the taxpayers, through their political representatives, agreeing to shoulder the burden of making good the losses of private business and of forgiving the debts of borrowing nations (in exchange for political and economic concessions from the debtors which may prevent them from ever emerging from bankruptcy)?

That, in a nutshell, is the dilemma which the Third World debt crisis presents.

2. The net transfer

The most widely known and used indicator of debt burdens is the *debt service ratio*. This is the relationship, expressed as a percentage, of the debt service payments (amortisation of capital plus interest) to the foreign exchange earnings of the country in question over a given time period (usually one year). Thus, a country which had export earnings of $1.5 billion dollars in 1986 and paid $300 million in debt service would have a debt service ratio of $300/$1500 or 20 per cent.

Although widely used,[15] the debt service ratio is almost totally useless as a predictor of debt servicing difficulties, except for the broad observation that the higher the ratio, the larger the problem.

The first reason this ratio has been useless is that no one, at least among lenders, seems to have used it as a guide to action. For the experts have never been able to agree on what the danger level is! 'There seems to be no critical level beyond which default may be expected.'[16]

In 1962, the World Bank suggested that 7 per cent was the maximum prudent debt service ratio.[17] In the 1960s, 10 per cent was commonly taken as significant. But significant of what? As the years went on, and the debt burdens climbed faster than the growth of the borrowers' economies, the ratios for several major borrowers exceeded 10 and climbed towards 20 per cent.

But even 20 per cent did not prove to be a barrier. Indeed, there seemed to be very little connection between the size of the ratio and actual debt-servicing difficulties. Algeria, for example, carried debt service ratios of over 30 per cent for several years in the early 1980s without failing to service its debt, while African countries with ratios under 10 per cent fell deeply into arrears.

Further back in history, Australia and Canada did not default during the 1930s, despite the fact that they had investment service ratios (which include profit remittances as well as debt service) of 44 and 37 per cent respectively.

Another problem with the debt service ratio is that its component elements are so unstable that trend lines cannot be established with any accuracy. The instability of commodity export prices introduced wild swings into the denominator, as did such elements as the earnings of migrant or emigrant workers (which was the largest single positive item of the balance of payments for India, Pakistan, Bangladesh and Sri Lanka in the late 1970s and early 1980s). The sharp rise in interest rates after 1981 combined with the synchronous decline in export prices caused a quantum leap in the ratio in the early 1980s, which indeed coincided with the debt crisis but did not predict it.

Conversely, a debt rescheduling could postpone the 'hump' of principal payments a few years into the future and 'improve' the debt service ratio without reducing the debt, indeed, even while increasing the total. The practice of rescheduling or rolling over the principal became so universal after 1982 that it is common now to use 'interest only' as the numerator of the ratio, an implicit admission that the principal will not be repaid in the foreseeable future.

The debt crisis caused another problem for the use of debt service ratios. When past statistics are compiled, these *ex post* ratios use the amount of debt service that was *actually paid* for the numerator. When projections are made for the future (*ex ante*) however, the figures given are for the amount of debt service that is *contractually due* but, in current circumstances, highly unlikely to be paid in full. The two series of figures, past and future, are therefore not comparable. Projections of future debt service due are inevitably understated, furthermore, if new debt is contracted after the projections are calculated.

The most serious problem with using the debt service ratio as an indicator of trouble, however, is that it fails to take into account new inflows of capital from creditors. A country which has a debt service ratio of 20 per cent may get along fairly well if it is at the same time receiving new loans which more than cover the outflow of debt service. Another country with the same 20 per cent ratio might find itself plunged into crisis if that 20 per cent actually has to be paid out of export earnings. These two countries may have identical export earnings and debt service ratios, but one country can use 100 per cent of its earnings, while the other can use only 80 per cent.[18]

It is because it takes account of this critical element of the inflow of new money that the *net transfer* is a superior indicator of crisis. The net transfer measures the relationship between new inflows of money and the debt service on previously incurred debt.

The administration of foreign aid and the study of economic development have produced hundreds of technical terms which are rarely encountered in the larger world. They have specific meanings which may not be readily apparent to the nonspecialist. The net transfer, a key element of the argument of this book, is calculated with the help of two other concepts, the gross flow and the net flow of funds across borders.

The *gross flow* is the total amount of new lending which is extended to all the borrowers within a country within a given time period (usually one year).

The *net flow* is the difference between the gross flow and the *repayment of principal* (which is also called amortisation) on old debt in that same time period.

The *net transfer* is the difference between the net flow and the payments of *interest* which are made in that time period.

gross flow	minus	repayment of principal	equals	net flow
net flow	minus	interest payments	equals	net transfer

Table 2.1
Latin America: Gross Capital Inflows, Debt Service, and Net Transfer of Resources, 1976–1983

	1976	*1977*	*1978*	*1979*	*1980*	*1981*	*1982*	*1983*
Gross disbursements (US$ million)	31,387	29,812	52,638	53,326	64,336	72,069	62,421	49,630
Amortization	8,551	11,791	16,913	21,108	19,475	21,426	27,758	27,760
Interest	6,643	7,711	10,870	16,745	21,128	32,527	38,545	39,051
Net transfer	16,193	10,310	24,855	15,473	20,733	18,116	–3,882	–17,181
Total debt service as percentage of gross disbursements	48	65	53	71	63	75	106	135
Interest as percentage of gross disbursements	21	26	21	31	33	45	62	79

Source: Adapted from *External Debt and Economic Development in Latin America*, Inter-American Development Bank, 1984, Table 4, page 19.

Figure 2.1
The Net Transfer for Latin America 1976–1983

Source: See attached table.

Data from Table 2.1 p. 12
Latin America: Capital inflows, debt service and net transfer of resources

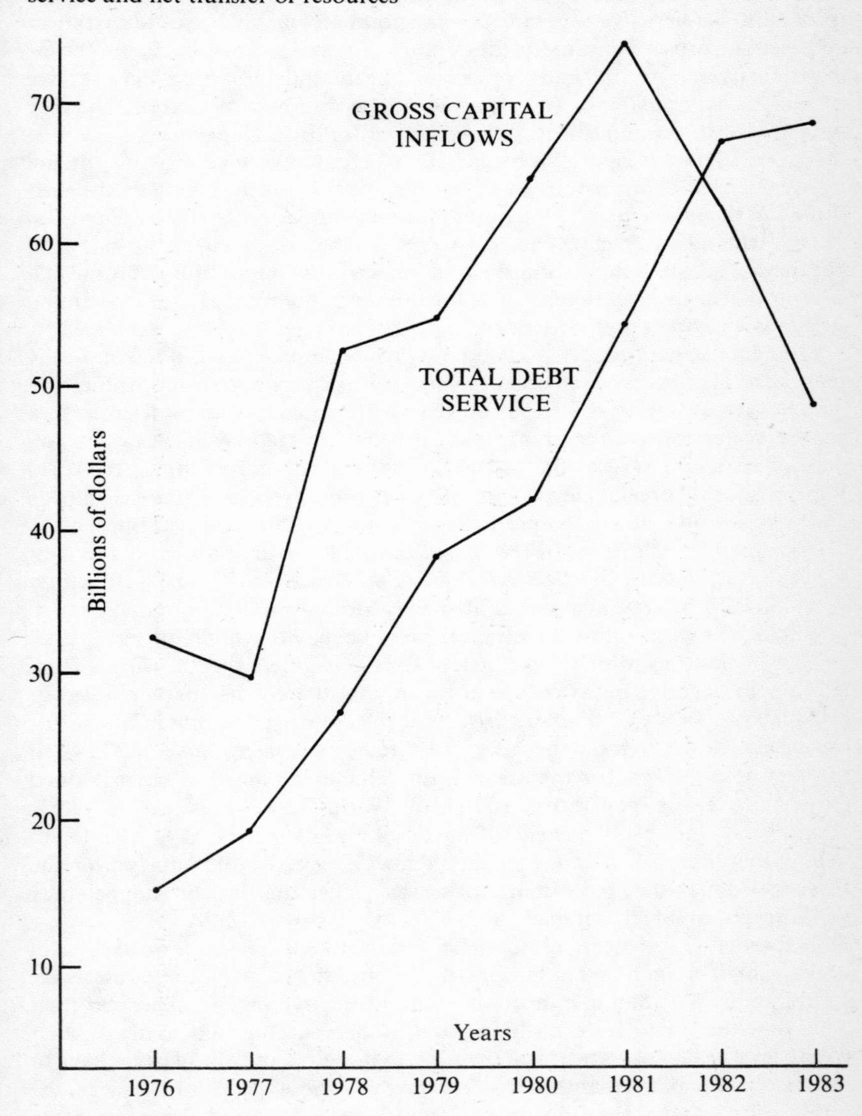

A negative net transfer may be triggered by a decline in new lending as well as by a rise in debt service; indeed both were present in 1982. Graph 2 illustrates the gross flow and total debt service for the major Latin American debtors between 1976 and 1983. The net transfer is the difference – first positive, then negative after 1982 – between the two amounts.

It is not just coincidence that X marks the beginning of the crisis. The transition to a negative net transfer – the point at which the ascending line of debt service crosses the line of descending (or more slowly ascending) new inflows – is a better indicator of crisis than the indeterminate 'debt service ratio'. The net transfer for all Latin America became negative in 1982, the year Argentina, Mexico and Brazil all shocked creditors by failing to meet scheduled payments. The African debt crisis cannot be dated so precisely but the net transfer to that continent became negative in 1984, which is roughly the time some African countries fell into arrears on their IMF repurchases (repayments). East Asia had a negative net transfer for the first time in 1986,[19] but this aggregate includes South Korea, which is the only major debtor which is able to run a large export surplus without forcing a sharply declining standard of living on its citizens.

The negative net transfer is a good but only an approximate indicator of the precise onset of crisis. Each country will have its own net transfer profile, and not every negative transfer indicates crisis. It could just as well indicate a healthy transition to an economy that can easily run trade surpluses and repay debts. Japan and Taiwan successfully negotiated that transition since World War II. South Korea achieved a negative net transfer/trade surplus as late as 1986 but has now begun to amortise its considerable foreign debt burden.

Additionally, the net transfer shares some of the limitations of the debt service ratio. Specifically, accurate figures are available (if ever) only with a delay of months or years; and neither indicator can accurately predict such psychological variables as the often irrational behaviour of creditors.

Those countries which have successfully navigated the transition from positive to negative net transfers illustrate that there is no mathematical or financial necessity that this will cause, or result from, a crisis. But in the case of most Third World debtors there does seem to be a strong *psychological* (as well as economic) reason for the association. That is because, as we explained earlier, an entire generation of Third World leaders, as well as their counterparts in the aid agencies of the developed countries, have been led to believe that their 'poor' countries should always receive more money from the First World than they pay out in debt service. When this does not happen they are outraged and feel betrayed.

In December 1986 the author participated in a conference on the Latin American debt in São Paulo, Brazil. Several speakers at the conference, including people holding important positions in government, expressed their view that there had been an 'unwritten' understanding that loans to their countries would always be rolled over, i.e. that their loans would never have to be paid. To the participants in that conference, who were mainly lawyers, the implication was that the obligation to repay loans was invalid if that unwritten understanding was not honoured.

Another example of 'net transfer' thinking was provided by the Finance Minister of Mexico, Jesús Silva Herzog, in August 1985. On the occasion of the signing ceremony for the supposedly pathbreaking Multi-Year Rescheduling Agreement (MYRA) which the banks had allowed Mexico (supposedly as a reward for good behaviour), Silva Herzog did not display the gratitude which the creditors might have expected. Instead he delivered a threat: if Mexico did not receive a positive net transfer of funds from the banks, it would not pay its interest in the future.

When Alan García, President of Peru, announced in 1985 that Peru would pay no more than 10 per cent of its export earnings on service of the public debt, he was using the traditional 'debt service ratio' indicator. But when some Peruvian economists advised him not to fall into arrears with the World Bank and the Inter-American Development Bank because Peru was still receiving more in new loans from those institutions than it was paying in debt service, they were using 'net transfer' reasoning.

The fact that the Third World (as a whole) has been shipping more money to the First World that it received from it since 1982 flies in the face of all the received wisdom of the postwar aid years. It means that for those nations, expenditures are not only limited by their own earnings, which their leaders hoped and believed would never happen, but that they are, in the words of Argentinian economist Aldo Ferrer, living *below* their means.[20]

It also means that it is past time to reconsider and challenge the received wisdom that has led into this trap.

3. The Ponzi scheme

Charles Ponzi was a con man who in 1919 persuaded investors that he could double their money in six months by purchasing International Postal Reply coupons in one country and redeeming them in another country where the exchange rate was higher. Within six months some 20,000 investors had put $10 million into his scheme. The first ones to invest did receive fabulously high returns, but they were paid with funds received from those who put their money in a little later. Ponzi had actually invested none of the receipts and the last wave of investors lost their money while he went to prison for fraud.[21]

Today a 'Ponzi scheme' denotes any scheme in which the original investors are paid off with money supplied by later investors. The same principle underlies 'pyramid schemes' and chain letters. It is essential to our understanding of the Third World debt crisis to know that it, too, operated like those confidence schemes.

Thousands of different creditor agencies and banks participated in Third World lending, and there were many differences among them. The rate of interest, the maturity of the loan, the grace period before repayment, policy conditions attached to the credit, the 'tying' of loans to goods made in particular countries or even to specific goods for an individual project – all these factors could be of great importance to a borrower, making one credit source more or less attractive than an alternative one.

But if we take a grand view of the total debt build-up over decades, the differences between hard and soft loans, public or private creditors, etc., seem less important than the features all loans have in common: the supply of money or credit at one point in time which has to be repaid at another, later, time. Therefore this chapter will examine how successive waves of these sources of credit have followed one another over the decades since the end of the Second World War in the grandest Ponzi scheme of all. It is a veritable fugue of rollovers, crises and bail-outs.

In previous chapters we explained the psychology of the net transfer – the belief on the part of both creditors and debtors that Third World economies were poor, short of capital and therefore 'natural' importers of capital. But no country has only a single creditor. Most debtor countries have dozens or even hundreds of creditors – the aid agencies of many different developed countries, the export credit agencies of most of these same countries, the World Bank, the regional development banks, the IMF and thousands of commercial banks based in many different countries. These creditors lend to many different borrowers at different points in time and with different interest rates and maturity dates.

From the point of view of the borrowing government, the completion of the cycle of lending by one creditor – who would take interest and eventually principal out of the country upon maturity of the loan – would predictably lead to a net transfer of funds out of the country *if that creditor were the only one*. But this seemed to be of no concern if other creditors were ready to step into the breach by making a new loan.

Thus, even if an individual creditor were not willing to roll over the principal of a loan, it could be achieved by the collective of lenders. The borrower would be in trouble only if new lenders could not be found to replace the ones withdrawing. An OECD study of the debt problem in 1974 concluded that the debt service ratio was not a satisfactory indicator of problems precisely because it did not take account of the rollover of principal. The amortisation of loans, the report stated, *globally* can be assumed to be rolled over through new borrowing.[22]

It is quite easy to build a model of multiple loans, with creditors 'rolling over' capital as repayments come due, and with new creditors stepping in to lend money as older creditors decide they want to take repayments and use the money elsewhere. (Indeed, as long as the debt is 'serviced' i.e. interest is paid, creditors would have no reason to wish to take out their money.) A model could be constructed using these assumptions which could overcome the 'negative net transfer' illustrated by graph 1 on pages 12–13.

This is exactly what most aid and capital flow specialists did when they thought about the debt problem. They constructed a model which assumed away the problem of servicing the debt. And for many years the world seemed to meet the assumptions of their models. But it was real-world creditors who had to put their own money on the line, and it finally became impossible to find enough old and new lenders who would fulfil the assumptions of the model.

A few debt experts built models which predicted trouble. Dragoslav Avramović, for example, who was the World Bank's first debt expert, constructed a table which illustrated the net transfer problem. Either debt service would quickly rise to the point where it exceeded net lending or *new* lending must rise steeply in order to maintain a stable net transfer.[23] Harry Magdoff published similar warnings.[24] Henry Bittermann, a retired US Treasury official, constructed an elaborate series of possible permutations of the debt service problem.[25] All of these models showed clearly that *either* debt service would soon overtake new lending and the net transfer would become negative, *or* gross lending would have to increase by stupendous amounts if a constant level of net transfer was to be maintained.

The widespread use of the 'debt service ratio' assumes that interest and principal will have to come out of the debtor country's export earnings. But as we have seen, there is a reluctance on the part of debtor governments to spend their own earnings on debt service, a reluctance that has been encouraged by the theories of mainstream development economists which hold that Third World countries are poor, short of capital, deficient in domestic savings and thus 'natural' importers of capital.

Given these assumptions, the safety of the *lenders'* capital was ultimately dependent not on the borrower's export earnings nor the power of the debtor government to tax its citizens but on *the willingness of new lenders to continue putting money into the country*. That is the definition of a Ponzi scheme.

Table 3.1
Gross and Net Borrowing and the Development of Debt Service with Hard Loan Terms — Two Time-patterns
(Loan terms: interest 6 per cent p.a., repayment over 15 years)

Year	*Annual gross borrowing*	*Debt outstanding*	*Annual amortization*	*Annual interest*	*Borrowing net of amortization*	*Transfer of resources net of interest and amortization*
a) Gross borrowing of 1000 per year						
5	1,000.0	4,333.0	266.8	216.0	733.2	517.2
10	1,000.0	6,998.5	600.3	395.9	399.7	3.8
15	1,000.0	7,996.5	933.8	475.8	66.2	–409.6
20	1,000.0	7,994.0	1,000.5	479.7	–0.5	–480.2
25	1,000.0	7,991.5	1,000.5	479.5	–0.5	–480.0
30	1,000.0	7,989.0	1,000.5	479.4	–0.5	–479.9
40	1,000.0	7,984.0	1,000.5	479.1	–0.5	–479.6
50	1,000.0	7,979.0	1,000.5	478.8	–0.5	–479.3
60	1,000.0	7,974.5	1,000.5	478.5	–0.5	–479.0
b) Transfer of resources of 1000 per year net of amortization and interest						
5	1,583.3	5,637.1	320.8	262.5	1,262.5	1,000.0
10	2,670.8	13,180.7	981.3	689.5	1,689.5	1,000.0
15	4,336.6	23,275.8	2,075.7	1,260.9	2,260.9	1,000.0
20	6,505.2	36,785.3	3,479.6	2,025.6	3,025.6	1,000.0
25	9,399.9	54,864.0	5,351.0	3,048.9	4,048.9	1,000.0
30	13,300.0	79,057.3	7,881.7	4,418.3	5,418.3	1,000.0
40	25,460.1	154,760.3	15,756.7	8.703.4	9,703.4	1,000.0
50	47,247.8	290,332.9	29,870.5	16,377.3	17,377.3	1,000.0
60	86,267.5	533,122.9	55,147.3	30,120.2	31,120.2	1,000.0

Source: IBRD Economic Department.

4. The transfer problem

The Marshall Plan was an enormous 'foreign aid' program extended to Europe in the years 1947–50. It affected the Third World only because the colonial powers in Europe used some of the money they borrowed for investment in their colonies – and for putting down anti-colonial wars and insurrections. The Marshall Plan did not leave a debt problem.

The Marshall Plan is nevertheless of great interest to a study of Third World debt precisely because it is the exception that proves the rule. It seems ironic that the easiest terms – grant aid – were extended to countries that needed reconstruction capital but could be expected to recover quickly to become industrial powers competing with their aid donor, the United States. But it was not ironic; it was precisely *because of* this expected competition that the Marshall Plan recipients were not required to repay the aid they received.[26]

Economists and policy-makers in the mid-1940s debated the consequences to the US economy of postwar foreign investment and lending. A major concern of this debate was the promotion and preservation of 'full employment' in the United States. Export markets abroad, it was hoped, would be a 'foreign contribution' to domestic full employment. 'A net foreign contribution to the aggregate demand for a country's output may be said to exist when there is an excess of exports over imports of current output (including services).'[27]

This idea of the 'foreign contribution' to US prosperity provides an interesting contrast to contemporary thinking about the function of the foreign aid program. At that time it was universally agreed that lending and investment abroad by the US government and private corporations could, in the short term, finance this 'foreign contribution'. But it was also recognised that the reverse flows of profit remittance and debt service which would be generated by such investment would soon create a 'transfer problem' for the United States. Although the terminology is confusingly similar, the 'transfer problem' is analytically distinct from the 'net transfer' discussed in Chapter 2. The 'transfer problem' refers to the international flow of real goods and services which are financed by flows of funds. The 'problem' is the competition to domestic producers presented by foreign goods. The United States would be required to accept in payment imports of goods and services that would compete with domestic business and threaten full employment.

> Probably the most disturbing problem connected with the investment of American capital abroad is that of the ultimate adjustment to the position of a mature creditor nation with receipts of income and principal in excess of new investment and with the balance on trade and service transactions adjusted to accommodate the change in investment items.[28]
>
> As long as new American investment abroad exceeds payments on outstanding foreign investment, the question of net repayment on our total foreign investment will not arise. But when net repayment eventually begins, it will involve an excess of imports of goods and services over exports. *Repayment in the form of imports has been traditionally opposed in this country on the ground that it causes competition for domestic producers and contributes to unemployment.* We are therefore faced with the alternatives of inviting defaults or adapting our economy to repayments in goods and services.[29]

The mention of traditional opposition to payment through imports referred to the enforcement of prohibitively high tariffs and other protectionist policies. While the inability of European and Latin American debtors to service debt in the 1930s was probably due more to the collapse of credit than to protectionism,[30] high tariffs were an indication of domestic political response to the threat that debts to the US might actually be repaid.

John Maynard Keynes satirised the attitude of the United States to its creditors in 1932:

> The rest of the world owes them money. They will not take payment in goods; they will not take it in bonds; they have already received all the gold there is. The puzzle which they have set to the rest of the world admits logically of only one solution, namely, that some way must be found of doing without their exports.[31]

Most economists agreed that accepting repayment of postwar loans and investments would threaten full employment and was for that reason unacceptable. They therefore examined what options were available to *avoid* repayment. One was to extend credit on a grant basis, the option eventually used in the Marshall Plan. 'Foreign giving involves no problem of interest or repayment, and can be continued indefinitely.'[32]

If loans were used, there were basically two choices. The first was 'lending in perpetuity'.

> There is only one way of indefinitely maintaining an export surplus on current account by foreign loans, and that is by lending interest as well as principal. Since interest is due from the borrower not only on the original principal sums but on the interest borrowed, *the net amount which must annually be lent to maintain a given export surplus must increase at a compound rate.*[33]

This was what had happened in the early part of the century, before the lending boom of the 1920s collapsed at the beginning of the 1930s. As the National Planning Association summarised that experience in a 1944 pamphlet:

> The dilemma posed by foreign desire to buy our goods and our own willingness to sell but not to buy abroad was temporarily 'solved' during the twenties by exporting capital to pay for our own exports and to refund debts and investment payable to us. In this way we were able to maintain exports at a level of 20 to 50 per cent above the import level. Some of these investments, however, were so worthless that, in effect, we gave away the money with which our exports were purchased.[34]

As another analyst explained, the only remaining option was to accept default.

> [I]t would be wholly logical to permit the waiver or deferment of [debt-service] payments in the event of a dollar shortage . . . [T]his would be desirable, not only in the interest of the debtor, *but also in the interest of the creditor* . . . [A]s an exporter, the United States also has an interest that, in times of strain, *service on investment should not have primacy over new production and the continued flow of merchandise trade*.[35]

In practice, all three of these options eventually came to the same thing: lending in perpetuity meant making 'investments' so worthless it was equivalent to giving it away, and was followed by default, which was a retroactive admission that the money had been given away. Some economists concluded from this that international lending was not a desirable option for maintaining full employment, and that America should cultivate its own market rather than conquering customers abroad.

> If we accept the view that international trade should be on a give-and-take basis, giving everybody a chance to do what he can do best, we cannot look to net export sales as a long-run use for savings.[36]

This was not to be the prevailing view, however.

In the late 1940s, economists understood and debated the trade implications of foreign investment and lending. For this reason Marshall Plan aid was extended in grant form precisely because it was recognised that *the United States did not want to receive the massive flow of goods from European factories which they would have been required to accept in repayment for the loans*. But subsequently, as the US program of foreign aid to the Third World got underway in the 1950s, the desirability of export surpluses was reaffirmed but the critical relationship between debt repayments and the invasion of US markets by foreign goods was forgotten.

The temptation of external markets was too great to resist in a postwar world that was at least temporarily hungry for American goods. And by 1950 economists were finding ways to rationalise the option of perpetual lending to the rest of the world. Four years after Hinshaw and Lary made their sober predictions, and in the same forum, the Annual Meeting of the American Economic Association, an optimistic presentation by E. D. Domar provided the justification for the pursuit of a perpetual economic surplus in a universe that was assumed to be constantly expanding. He was explicitly trying to refute the pessimism of Hinshaw and others, like Jacob Viner, who thought that 'for American employment to be sustained for any length of time by American capital export there would be needed an outward gross flow of capital increasing every year at an increasing rate of increase and eventually reaching fantastic levels.'[37] Domar was more optimistic:

> It should at least be possible to equalise the rate of growth and interest on public investment alone by the simple expedient of raising the rate of growth of new loans to the level of the interest rate charged. The inflow and outflow of government funds will then gradually balance, and a revolving fund will come into existence . . .[38]

Domar modestly insisted that he was only working out the mathematical possibilities, but his work endorsed Hinshaw's option of lending in perpetuity – 'lending interest as well as principal', while making the sums needed sound less scary than Hinshaw and Viner had implied. (His model of the revolving fund also necessarily implied that the 'foreign contribution' would eventually stagnate without further growth, even if it did not reverse.) This comforting reassurance that the US need never suffer an import surplus or the need to cease investing overseas was echoed in the *Report to the President on Foreign Economic Policies* (the Grey Report):

> The servicing of development loans will generally not cause trouble in the future if we achieve the goal of an expanding free world economy, and the reasonable flow of such investment that the expanding economy requires.[39]

And so US economists embarked on the odyssey of wishful thinking – of assuming away precisely those problems that should be examined – that was to culminate thirty years later in the Third World debt crisis.

5. The rich and the poor

It is instructive to look back to the 1950s and 1960s to see how the 'need' for capital imports was justified by economists and policy-makers to themselves and to the general public. With the benefit of hindsight we will be particularly interested as well in the way in which each of these theorists handled the problem of future repayments.

As we have seen, the need for export of capital in the 1940s was frankly admitted to be a US problem, even though at the same time the United States expected gratitude from the recipients.

A 1950 article by the British/Australian economist Colin Clark argued for extension of the Marshall Plan concept to what would in future be known as the Third World. Clark's scheme divided the world into those countries which had excess savings and those with deficient savings capacities. The problem of the rich countries he described as follows:

> It is now becoming easier to see the contrasting dangers that threaten the welfare of the richer and the poorer countries; in the one, a capacity to save in excess of the opportunities for remunerative industrial investment within the country, which must therefore either express itself in international investment, or must be squandered in budget deficits, or else if left alone will lead to devastating unemployment.[40]

In the poorer countries, on the other hand,

> . . . [W]e see strenuous but fruitless efforts to accumulate from their own small resources sufficient capital to provide for a reasonable rate of economic progress; and in attempting this impossible objective they tend to impose drastic governmental control of foreign trade and of internal economic life, tending all the while to autarkic totalitarianism.[41]

Clark expanded the concept of surplus countries to include not only the United States but also the other rapidly recovering industrial economies. And in case readers had missed his first attempt to portray the horrors of affluence, he underlined the subject a second time:

> The surplus countries – that is to say, the US and the British dominions almost immediately, Western Europe and Japan as soon as war damage is overtaken – will find themselves with a capacity to produce goods well beyond their natural internal requirements for consumption and investment. If they are unwilling or unable to invest abroad they must either resign themselves to a state of chronic depression and unemployment (as the US did during the 1930s) or else rely on artificial manipulation of government spending and public finance to stimulate consumption by social service recipients or investment in more or less unwanted public works . . .
>
> *Such a policy would also mean a disastrous loss of markets for industries hitherto depending upon exports.*[42]

Clark submitted calculations of projected savings surpluses or deficits for all the major areas of the world, presented in pretty coloured charts in *Fortune* where the article was published. He proposed that the central banks of the world get together in what he termed a World Bank (a new construction; not the one founded at Bretton Woods) where they would exchange surpluses among themselves with a minimum of political or bureaucratic interference. The way in which he dealt with the question of repayment was emblematic for the three decades which followed: an utterly confused amalgam of wishful thinking and insistence on the sanctity of contract. 'Something like the present debtor–creditor relationships may prevail for twenty years or more, and any attempt to force premature payment would be disastrous.'[43] Disastrous for whom, he does not say, though we can infer from the extracts quoted above that it would be disastrous for the rich countries as well as for the poor.

> On the other hand, any attempt to make the creditor countries leave their money in the bank forever would be dishonest. Over a period of time [the longer the better? we are tempted to add – CP] as the borrowing countries developed, the repayment of their credits would be provided for. The fact it was organised through a World Bank should make it about as safe and attractive an investment as any that can be contemplated.[44]

Colin Clark thus became one of the first economists to propose massive transfers of funds to the poor countries for the purpose of economic development. Unlike the American economists of the immediate postwar period, he seemed to be equally as concerned with the needs of the poor countries as he was with the needs of the surplus countries. And like the economists who followed this path and built formal models justifying the lending, he airily fudged the question of repayment.

6. Myths and models

> Models which though complex are built out of a small number of elements that are assumed but are not known to be representative of the predominant tendencies of the real world are no help to those who have to diagnose and prescribe for the actual economy.[45]

Economists' models are like fairy tales. In fairy tales, the princess is always beautiful, the prince is always brave, and the third (and youngest) child always solves the problem.

In economists' models the myths are similarly unworldly. Resources are always fully employed, and always allocated efficiently. Competition is always perfect, likewise information. Even more, we have perfect *foresight* for many years into the future, and *ceteris* is always *paribus*.

There are only two nations, two factors of production, and two commodities. And politics has nothing to do with these eternal truths.

Anything can be proved with a model if the right assumptions are specified. Models do have their place, but their limitations must be recognised. In particular, we must guard against the temptation to build models which specify the outcome we would like to see, and then assume that behaviour in the real world will conform to the assumptions which we have built into the model to make it come out right.

Prodded by the anti-war movement, the economics profession passed briefly through a self-critical phase in the early 1970s, in which the more honest souls admitted these problems:

> By the time it comes to interpretation of the substantive conclusions, the assumptions on which the model has been based are easily forgotten. But it is precisely the empirical validity of these *assumptions* on which the usefulness of the entire exercise depends.[46]

In the economic literature on international capital flows, two models have had a disproportionate influence on thinking about foreign aid and foreign capital flows. One of these was produced by Paul Rosenstein-Rodan,[47] an associate of Max Millikan and W. W. Rostow at the Massachusetts Institute of Technology's Center for International Affairs, whose contribution to the mythology of foreign aid is detailed in Chapter 9.

The key assumptions in Rosenstein-Rodan's article are:

- Foreign capital will be a pure addition to domestic capital formation, i.e. it will all be invested, and
- The investment will be productive or 'businesslike' and result in increased production.

> The main function of foreign capital inflow is to increase the rate of domestic capital formation up to a level . . . which could then be maintained without any further aid.[48]
>
> Absorptive capacity relates to the ability to use capital productively. While not every single investment project need be 'self-liquidating', total investment must not only cover its costs but must also yield a reasonable increase in income.[49]

Rosenstein-Rodan softened the latter assumption, however, when he considered the problem of repayment. His solution to the problem was to avoid it by specifying, as the vehicle of capital flow, either grants (with no repayment expectation) or loans of such long terms that the repayment period is pushed off to another generation.

> *Capacity to repay*. The foreign capital inflow mobilized by international action should be within the limits on one hand of technical absorptive capacity, and on the other hand of the *capacity to repay* of underdeveloped countries. While the first limit should preponderantly determine the amount of aid, the second limit should largely determine the method of financing it. Where the capacity to repay in low-income underdeveloped countries is below their absorptive capacity, a proportion of aid will have to be given in grants or 'soft loans', 40–99 year loans with a ten to twenty years' grace period and a low rate of interest, or loans repayable in local currency which will be relent for subsequent investment.[50]

Indeed, he suggests that countries need never repay principal at all:

> It is by no means rational for each country to reduce its foreign indebtedness to zero. The rational question to ask is: 'How much foreign indebtedness can a country maintain in the long run?' After ten to twenty years of aid the net capital inflow to underdeveloped countries will come to a stop. The gross capital inflow, however, will continue, while at the same time old loans will be repaid. In exactly the same way in which any national debt (or corporate debt) need not be reduced if it is within sound limits, the foreign debt of debtor countries need not be amortized to zero in a sound world economy.[51]

One more key phrase must be noted. Rosenstein-Rodan (using Rostow's terminology)[52] defined *self-sustaining growth* as 'a stage where aid is not required any more, while normal capital imports – private foreign investment – may continue.'

This definition of 'self-sustaining growth' was generally accepted among the capital flow theorists. The World Bank's chief debt expert, for example, wrote in 1964 that

> Self-sustained growth is defined to mean a rate of income increase of, say, 5% p.a. financed out of domestically generated funds and *out of foreign capital which flows into the country because it wants to do so.*[53]

And yet another international economics specialist, writing about 'self-sustaining' development: 'Such countries should be able to maintain their growth rates with the aid of external capital obtained from nonconcessionary sources.'[54]

Rosenstein-Rodan thus appeared to prescribe the successful borrowing pattern as progress from net borrowing to a steady-state condition where loans would be rolled over rather than repaid, and/or as progression from concessional to market finance. *He assumes throughout no net repayment of debt.*

In the article he also provided predictions of the years in which various countries would reach the stage of 'self-sustaining growth' thus defined. With hindsight it makes interesting reading:
Colombia: 1965
Argentina and Mexico: sometime 1965–75
India: early 1970s
Pakistan: three to five years later than India
Philippines: after 1975
Yugoslavia: 1966
Greece: end of 1960s.

The most interesting thing about this list is that most of these countries did switch, at least partially, to commercial borrowing, at roughly the dates predicted or even earlier (India could have but chose not to borrow commercially in the 1970s). What he did not predict was what would come *after* the graduation to commercial borrowing.

The second influential economic model was published five years later by Hollis Chenery and Alan Strout.[55] The major departure from the previous Rosenstein–Rodan model (which it otherwise confirmed and complemented) was the discovery of a 'foreign exchange gap' which supplemented the 'savings gap' as a justification for foreign borrowing. The 'foreign exchange gap' arises, according to this model, from the successful pursuit of economic growth. If the domestic economy grows faster than export earnings, the economy's 'propensity to import' will result in a shortage of foreign exchange and the consequent inability to import production goods which are necessary to the continued growth of the economy. In other words, as shown in the next chapter, domestic economic growth tends to worsen rather than improve balance of payments problems.

'Donors and recipients now agree that economic and social development is their primary objective', Chenery and Strout assert rather defensively.[56] In fact, there is no reason to believe that there was any more agreement on the objective of pure economic development in 1966 than there was in 1964 when Chenery had asserted that 'the main objective of foreign assistance, as of many other tools of foreign policy, is to produce the kind of political and economic environment in the world in which the United States can best pursue its own social goals.'[57] Indeed, as the US government shipped hundreds of thousands of troops to Vietnam, the suspicion must be that economic and social development was even less in 1966 than previously an end in itself.

The Chenery–Strout model is highly technical and mathematical. We will not attempt a critique of its mathematics but instead will search for the underlying assumptions, which are critical to any model. And first, it must be said that the assumptions of this model are not given explicitly but are buried deep in the text or in footnotes or must be inferred. But when we find them, we can see that several of the most critical assumptions are counterfactual: that is, they are contradicted by the actual state of affairs in the real world.

First, they assume that availability of external markets is no constraint, an assumption that must be questioned in the age of protectionist barriers in all the major rich-country markets: more so in Japan and the EEC, less in the United States but of growing importance.

Second, they assume that import substitution is a permissible option as a means to control the need for imports.[58] And yet the International Monetary Fund has always made the elimination of import and exchange controls, the primary tools of import substitution, the main objective of the conditions it imposes for use of its loans. (See Chapter 12.)

Even as this influential article was published, a large and expensive propaganda machine which endeavoured to 'prove' that import substitution harmed economic growth was being geared up. In the next decade, three separate but not really independent multi-volume, multi-country research projects would reach nearly identical conclusions condemning import substitution.[59] More importantly, the conclusions gave ideological support to policy prescriptions that were backed up by threats of withholding aid and other capital flows.

Although the honesty of the findings of these projects has been questioned,[60] the international financial organisations and what might be called the international financial establishment (what became, at the outbreak of the debt crisis, the creditors' cartel) have subscribed to the anti-import substitution conclusion with monolithic uniformity, making import liberalisation a condition not just for aid and for IMF programs but for any type of debt relief as well.

Whether one agrees or not with the findings of these research projects or the wisdom of IMF conditionality, one important assumption of the Chenery–Strout model which justifies foreign capital inflows is in practice not available to borrowing countries, because the inflows are made conditional on renunciation of import substitution as a tool or as a goal.

The core assumptions of the Chenery–Strout model have been criticised by several respected economists.[61] Economist Keith Griffin has systematically challenged the basic assumption of the model: that foreign capital is additional to domestic saving and thus increases the amount and the productivity of investment.

Griffin and a co-author demonstrated from statistical data on several Latin American countries that 'the greater the capital inflow from abroad, the lower the rate of growth of the receiving country,' and from time-series data on Turkey that the relationship between the increase in GNP *per capita* and the amount of foreign aid received was actually negative. Then they asked 'Why may there be an inverse relationship between foreign assistance and growth?'

> In the usual models with which economists deal, such a result is impossible. These models visualize capital imports as having two effects: (a) increasing the level of investment directly by the amount of the aid and (b) increasing the rate of capital accumulation indirectly by raising the level of income and . . . the rate of internal savings. Thus it is imagined that all aid is invested, and this leads not only to a higher rate of capital accumulations but also to a larger proportion of income being saved.
>
> For example, in the 'basic model' of Chenery and Strout the constraint on growth is assumed to be savings . . . Chenery and Strout assume the recipient country is 'unwilling or unable to increase aid merely to increase consumption' and they believe recipient governments have 'no incentive . . . to increase aid by reducing savings'.
>
> These are extremely odd assumptions. Foreign and domestic savings are substitutable resources. In effect, models of the Chenery–Strout type make domestic savings depend upon GNP or alternatively, upon national income per capita, rather than on total available resources. Yet as long as the cost of aid (e.g. the rate of interest on foreign loans) is less than the incremental output–capital ratio, it will 'pay' a country to borrow as much as possible and substitute foreign for domestic savings. In other words, given a target rate of growth in the developing country, foreign aid will permit higher consumption, and domestic savings will simply be a residual, that is, the difference between desired investment and the amount of foreign aid available. Thus the foundations of models of the Chenery–Strout type are weak, since one would expect, on theoretical grounds, to find an inverse association between foreign aid and domestic savings.[62]

In practice, this expectation is fulfilled. Private entrepreneurs need not restrict their own consumption if loans are available from abroad. Governments are enabled to substitute foreign funds for tax increases or badly needed reforms in tax collections. Griffin and Enos even quote Chenery himself to this effect: [In Latin America] 'aid has been a substitute for savings, not an addition to investment. The savings rate has not increased and there has been no increase in the overall rate of growth of the gross national product.'[63]

Griffin also dismisses the second 'gap' of the Chenery–Strout model, that of foreign exchange.

> In the long run – and the analytic basis of these gaps is a long-run growth model – no economy is so rigid that it can neither produce capital goods, nor export goods nor import substitutes. It is possible, of course, that a government is unwilling rather than unable to introduce policies which would earn or save foreign exchange. In such a case it might appear that foreign exchange is the binding constraint, but it is the unwillingness to reduce domestic consumption in order to expand exports or reduce imports which is the source of the difficulty.[64]

To those unfamiliar with the commitment of Griffin to egalitarian development,[65] this prescription may sound harsh and lacking in compassion for the suffering induced by severe foreign exchange shortages. In fact, had his warnings about the dangers of capital import been heeded, they could have abated the severity of the present shortages since, as has been emphasised, debt service on previous foreign borrowing, and not the original 'capital scarcity' of the economy in question, is the cause of the present severity.

Like most other economists in the field of aid, Chenery and Strout did not define self-sustaining growth as growth achieved on the basis of a country's own resources aided only by a balanced international trade, but as 'graduation' from 'aid' to market-rate flows of foreign capital: self-sustaining growth was defined in their article as 'growth at a given rate with capital inflows limited to a specified ratio to GNP which can be sustained without *concessional* financing.'[66]

Like Rosenstein–Rodan, these two authors named a few of the countries they believed to be 'successfully completing the transition' to market-rate finance. They were Israel, Greece, Taiwan, Mexico, Peru and the Philippines; the last three in time became basket cases of Third World debt. Like most of the theorists we have quoted in this chapter, Chenery and Strout apparently believed that the graduation to commercial finance represented the fairy-tale ending of living happily ever after. Like all but a very few Cassandras who were not heeded, they did not worry about the repayment of debt.

It is tempting to judge these tremendously influential theorists harshly, because by lending theoretical respectability to the idea that foreign capital is almost always beneficial in its effects they created the intellectual climate in which commercial finance was welcomed and the Ponzi scheme built to a dizzying height. This might be unfair as we do have the advantage of hindsight over those who published these works in the 1960s. We should, however, not forgive those, whether the same people or their *epigone*, who persist in believing the same fairy tales in the 1990s, years after the inflow of foreign finance has created its own inevitable and predictable drain of capital.

7. Economic growth and the balance of payments

> Any country that, over the long term, is a net importer of goods will eventually run out of both dollars and the ability to borrow them, and it is therefore a bad credit risk. Period.[67]
>
> [T]here is not a normal sequence through which an economy must move from young debtor to mature creditor over a given span of time. The notion that such a sequence exists was drawn from US experience, but it fits few other countries.[68]

Another model cited as a justification for international capital flows to poor countries is the theory of balance-of-payments 'stages' which a 'young' country is presumed to pass through on its path to developed nation status.[69]

It is generally assumed (and not only by economists) that capital imports contribute to growth, from which the external debt can be serviced. The conventional wisdom is that it can and should be, but reality has not conformed to theory.

In order to understand why, we must consider the meaning of the word 'growth'.

Take as an example a private firm producing shoes for the domestic market in a Latin American country, which has borrowed working capital both in domestic currency from a local bank and in foreign currency from a US bank. If the shoe company invests wisely, expands its production, and is able to sell shoes at a profit which exceeds its debt service, it will be able to pay its *domestic* creditors without problems.

But repaying its foreign debt is more complicated. The firm must take its earnings, in domestic currency, to the central bank and exchange it for dollars. Its ability to repay will depend not only on its business skills and success but also on two other factors: firstly, the exchange rate, or the amount of domestic currency it will need in order to buy foreign exchange needed to service the debt; secondly, the central bank's ability to collect sufficient foreign exchange to satisfy all such demands from its domestic industries.

In the time between contracting and repaying the foreign loan, the domestic equivalent of the borrowed money, and more, has been paid out in wages, purchases from suppliers, debt service and profits. A number of people have increased their earnings thanks to the growth of the shoe company. All of them will spend some of their extra income on imports: *how much* they spend on imports will depend on the relative price of domestic and foreign goods and whether the government has imposed controls on imports.[70]

In an open economy, that is, one without exchange and import controls, every rise in domestic growth will usually result in a rise in imports. In other words, if our shoe factory does not earn enough dollars to pay its foreign debts from shoe exports, its growth will result in a net drain of dollars from the national economy. If a great number of firms are producing for the domestic market while their workers, suppliers and stockholders are spending a portion of their higher incomes on imports, the result will be a foreign exchange crisis and the firm may not be able to obtain the dollars it needs for its debt service from the central bank.

In other words (all other things being equal) *growth stimulated by the domestic market tends to cause or intensify balance of payments problems rather than solving them.*

Alternatively, the firm might decide to export part of its production. Export-led growth, if successful, does produce foreign exchange earnings. But in order to service and repay debts, countries must be able to do two things: find markets which will accept import surpluses of the necessary magnitude; and moderate their own import demand to allow the necessary current account surplus. As we have pointed out, the developed countries, as a matter of policy, do not wish to provide expanded markets for their trading partners or reduce exports to them. As we shall see when we consider International Monetary Fund conditionality, they are not willing to permit import or exchange controls for IMF clients. Such a reversal of capital (and real resource) flows would be painful for both debtor and creditor. Historically, this has seldom been accomplished without financial crashes, defaults and/or wars.

Paul Samuelson's widely used college textbook on economics has been extremely influential in propagating the idea that there are 'natural' balance of payments stages through which any country must pass as it develops.[71]

> Historically, the United States has gone through the four stages typical of growth of a young agricultural nation into a well-developed industrialized one . . .
>
> 1. Young and growing debtor nation. From the Revolutionary War until after the Civil War, we imported on current account more than we exported. England and Europe lent us the difference in order to build up our capital structure . . .
>
> 2. Mature debtor nation. From about 1873 to 1914, our balance of trade appears to have become favourable. But growth of the dividends and interest that we had to pay abroad on our past borrowing kept our balance on current account more or less in balance. Capital movements were also nearly in balance, our new lending just about cancelling our borrowing.

So far, so good, except for the fact that other sources on the US balance of payments suggest that the United States was actually a net borrower only in the 1830s and again in the period 1850–73.[72]

> 3. New creditor nation. In World War I we expanded our exports tremendously . . . We emerged from the war as a creditor nation.

The question arises here: how easy would the transition to creditor have been had there not been a war which forced the Americans' major creditors to run their assets down rapidly and then contract new debt? Is war (between other countries) the solution to a debt problem? (Latin America's experience in World War II would lend some support to this provocative hypothesis).

The story gets more complicated at this point. Samuelson is forced to admit that the United States has in fact not played the proper role of creditor nation as prescribed by the stages theory.

> But our psychological frame of mind has not adjusted itself to our new creditor position. We passed high tariff laws in the 1920s and in 1930. Because we refused to import, foreigners found it difficult to get the dollars to pay us interest and dividends, much less repay principal.[73]
>
> So long as we remained in this third stage of being a new creditor country – so long, that is, as we kept making *new* private foreign loans all through the 1920s – everything momentarily appeared all right on the surface. We could continue to sell more than we were buying, by putting most of it 'on the cuff. . .' But by 1929 and later, when Americans would no longer lend abroad, the crash finally came. International trade broke down. Debts were defaulted. America, as much as the rest of the world, was to blame.
>
> 4. Mature creditor nation. England reached this stage some years ago, and as in such cases, her merchandise imports exceeded her exports . . . America has moved into the mature stage, where our earnings from abroad help finance our net imports from abroad and also our aid and security programs. Past capital movements are responsible for these vital investment earnings.[74]

Samuelson's elaboration of the four stages of successful borrowing is important in two respects. First, it illustrates that the United States was just as unwilling before World War II to accept the imports implied by the repayment of debt owed to it as it was after the war to accept repayment from Europe of Marshall Plan credit or to accept repayment in real goods and services from the Third World today.

Secondly, and more dangerously, this listing of 'stages' is important because it has been uncritically accepted as part of the justification for lending to the Third World. That is, it is argued that just as the United States, as a 'young' country, needed to borrow in order to grow, so the hundred-plus 'young' countries collectively known as the Third World should borrow to promote their own growth. This argument ignores the complexities of actual US history and the many differences between that history and the situation of borrowing countries today.

The U.S. borrowing process was, for example, by no means smooth. Unlike the postwar experience of most of the Third World, the United States did not borrow continuously, year after year. A few years of borrowing were interrupted by several years of payments surpluses, which reduced the debt before the next wave of borrowing.

Foreign capital was not judged to be especially productive; just the contrary, argues one historian:

> Until the last quarter of the nineteenth century, both government bonds and railway securities, the principal consumers of foreign capital, were *less* productive, pound for pound, franc for franc, dollar for dollar, than domestic investment; foreign capital was channelled deliberately into the kind of unproductive investment that could not be expected to attract the home investor.[75]

Nor did the transitions from years of trade deficits and borrowing to years of what are significantly called 'favourable' trade balances occur smoothly and without disruption. They were marked by defaults which had to be swallowed by the European creditors and by crashes and depressions in the United States and other borrowers.

> The crisis of 1873 was world-wide. It began in May with a panic in Vienna, extended to Germany and England, and in September broke out in New York. European lending ceased, railroad construction was halted, prices fell to a point where imports must diminish and exports expand. In 1874, for the first time since 1862, exports exceeded imports. Before 1874 the balance of trade had been generally unfavourable; from that year on, the balance has been favorable except in three years, 1875, 1888, and 1893. The year thus marks a turning point in our foreign trade.[76]

The nineteenth century was pockmarked with panics (for example, 1836, 1857, 1873 and 1893) followed by depression and accompanied, despite the enormous and undisputed natural wealth of the United States, by defaults or moratoria on debt payments. The Congress refused to assume responsibility for unpaid state obligations. The creditors were private investors who had no option but to accept their losses when loans were defaulted, while the defaulting borrowers apparently suffered only temporarily, if at all, from the ruin of their credit rating.[77]

Also ignored is the fortuity of World War I which allowed the United States and noncombatant countries, to make the transition from debtor to creditor rapidly and painlessly because the major creditor countries consumed huge amounts of imports while their productive capacity was diverted or destroyed.

Nor is it at all clear that 'foreign capital' played an essential or even positive role in the development of other countries. It is generally believed in Norway, for example, that the country's economic development was heavily dependent on capital imports for most of the past century. Yet when economist Ole David Koht Norbye looked at his country's foreign trade and debt statistics from 1865 to 1985 he discovered that although foreign borrowing had been heavy in the twenty-five year period before World War I, on balance 'the country has not had any very sizeable inflow of foreign capital in the long run.'[78]

In countries that did borrow heavily, the consequences were not always pleasant.

> [In Australia] There was the usual state borrowing for railways which was soundly enough based, but the bank borrowing was mad. When the 1890 Argentine Baring crisis tightened the London market the Australian banking structure collapsed and of 32 banks only 10 survived. In the 1890s the credit rating of Australia was so damaged that the state could not borrow money in London to finish railway lines.[79]

The length of time for which any country can sustain a foreign trade deficit depends, of course, on the size of that deficit and on other factors. It is difficult, however, to find any nation that has been able to borrow continuously for over twenty-five years without intervening periods of surpluses with which the debt is paid off or at least paid down. It is perhaps not just coincidence that it was exactly twenty-five years between the establishment of the US Development Loan Fund in 1957, on the occasion of which Secretary of State John Foster Dulles announced that 'Economic development is hereafter made through loans and not through grants,'[80] and the outbreak of the debt crisis in 1982.

We must also not forget that, far from being 'new' countries in the late twentieth century, the Latin American nations gained their independence in the 1820s and were importers of capital contemporaneously with the United States, raising the capital for many of the same 'productive' purposes (railroads, export agriculture) and suffering many of the same cycles of boom and bust as the United States.

Because some foreign capital was invested, and the country did develop, it does not follow that the foreign investment 'caused' or was necessary to the development. This is the *post hoc, ergo propter hoc* fallacy. It seems more likely that the causation worked in the opposite fashion: because foreign investors saw that a country was developing rapidly, they wanted to 'get in on the ground floor'. The effect of making foreign investment available might be to lower slightly the cost of capital, but its absence would not doom the process.

> Given that foreign finance never reached the dimensions so often attributed to it, was it not, nevertheless, disproportionately influential? Is it the 'margin' that counts? Was foreign finance of 'critical importance' (during the period covered by this book [1815–70]). *Autres temps, autres mores*, but the answer could be 'no'.[81]

The entire concpet of 'stages' is deceptive when applied to the balance of payments. Because deficits and surpluses of all countries on the globe must add up to zero every year (a 'zero-sum game'), it is logically impossible for every country to complete the course at the same time. Nor is the fourth stage necessarily the last. The US now appears to be in a fifth stage, which we might characterise as 'degenerate debtor'. Australia, Canada and South Africa are all struggling with large foreign debts that depress their ability to spend for other needs.

The four stages model is a *description* of *successful* borrowing strategies but corresponds to real-world countries only in a few cases. Only one of the heavily indebted Third World countries, South Korea, has accomplished even the transition to the second stage thus far.[82] A country cannot by itself guarantee that external markets for its exports will be there when the transition from the second to the third stage requires them. And even the United States, as Samuelson is frank enough to point out, has not always accepted the obligations presumed by the model.

In the first section, we have introduced several concepts which should help the reader to follow the recent history of international aid and credit presented in the next part of this book. The 'net transfer' refers to the difference between what a country receives in new lending and what it pays (interest *and* principal) to service old debts in a given period. The 'breakeven point' is the time at which a positive net transfer (excess of new borrowing over debt service) becomes negative (debt service exceeds new loans) and a country must service its debts out of its own earnings. The net transfer can be calculated for a single lender or for all lenders together.

When old lenders receive debt service funded by new borrowing, we are justified in comparing the collective operation to the investment scam called a Ponzi scheme. But the models developed by economists justified the flow of funds from creditor to debtor countries by assuming, despite a lack of empirical support, that the borrowed funds would eventually finance enough growth of productive power to cover the debt service. The lending countries, however, preferred to run export surpluses and were not inclined to assume the duties of a mature creditor nation: accepting the import surpluses necessary to enable the debtors to service the debts. The 'transfer problem' refers to the competitive threat which this import surplus poses for the domestically based economy and domestic labour of the creditor country.

Part Two: History

In this middle section, we follow the evolution of the Ponzi scheme of Third World debt through a rough chronology of the postwar decades, utilising the concepts and topics introduced in Part One and introducing new ones as necessary. The 1940s and 1950s are covered in the first three chapters, including an analysis of the Cold War aims of foreign aid programs. The next three chapters discuss some relevant features of the 1960s; the Alliance for Progress, the Paris Club and debt rescheduling; and the signals of impending crisis at the end of the decade.

Five chapters are devoted to the commercial bank lending of the 1970s. We show that the role of the OPEC 'price shock' has been exaggerated and misinterpreted, and demonstrate that the role of officials of the United States government and of the IMF and World Bank bear heavy responsibility for encouraging the lending bubble.

Finally, the last three chapters of the section form a critique of the successive 'plans' with which the creditors' cartel met the debt crisis they had done so much to cause (but had not been able to predict).

8. Ponzi finance in the early postwar decades

Amazingly enough, Latin America, or most of the countries in that area, *were facing a debt crisis at the end of each of the past three decades: the 1950s, the 1960s, and the 1970s.* It was only in the early 1980s that the crisis actually broke into public awareness: Ponzi scheme finance had rescued the situation in each of the two previous decades.

Stephany Griffith-Jones has elegantly described the model of Ponzi financial flows to Latin America:

> During each of the decades after the war a new actor arose, whose financial flows to Latin America played a major or dominant role in providing foreign exchange. In the 1950s it was the foreign investors pursuing greater profits who provided the main source of finance. During the 1960s official agencies played the most dynamic role as, in this decade, aid was perceived to be in the interests of industrialized countries, particularly the US. During the 1970s, the most dynamic actor was private bank credit, as at the time it was in the multinational banks' interests to expand their lending rapidly to several Latin American countries . . .
>
> In each decade the flows were initiated mainly by institutions or enterprises based in the US, and then the process became 'multinationalized' as institutions or enterprises from other countries increased their share in international capital markets.[83]

Clearly, the process described fits the classic definition of a Ponzi scheme, in which profits are paid with the proceeds of fresh money from newer investors:

> In the 1960s and 1970s the new flows helped service the outflows from the previous decade . . .[84]
>
> In the 1960s it could therefore be said that the net inflows of official finance were used up entirely to pay for the net outflow related to private direct investment.[85]
>
> In the 1970s an important proportion of total private bank lending serviced payments of profit remittances by foreign investors, interest and amortization of official debt and, increasingly, the private credits themselves.[86]

During World War II, most Third World countries, whether independent or still colonies, had accumulated large foreign exchange reserves by selling goods to the warring powers. After the war, when the developed countries began producing and exporting again, these societies began to spend their reserves on imports. The merchandise trade deficit was not the only cause of debt, but in the early years it was important.

Lending to Third World countries was negligible in the 1940s. Latin American countries first spent the large reserves they had accumulated during the war to pay for their excess of imports over exports. Most of Africa was still not independent, and Latin America was presumed to need only private foreign investment in the way of capital, supplemented by a few World Bank loans for projects which were designed to promote and support private direct investment, domestic and foreign. Even the World Bank only very cautiously began to extend credit to those countries towards the end of the decade.

In 1950s, the July newsletter of National City Bank noted that 'for the first time since 1946 the Latin American countries have been earning more than they have spent.' But the export credits of the following decade allowed them once again to run an import surplus. In the four years 1947–50, Mexico imported $2.256 billion worth of goods and exported $1.770 billion. Brazil had a small export surplus of $160 million in the same period. But both countries ran trade deficits in the 1950s: Mexico imported 38 per cent more by value than it exported, and Brazil imported 6 per cent more than it exported.

The first postwar mode of financing trade deficits (after national reserves were exhausted) were export credits, *both public and private*. Manufacturers or merchants who wanted to expand their markets in Latin America or other areas of the Third World extended credit themselves, or got export credit financing from government agencies such as the US Export–Import Bank (now known as Eximbank).

These debts were the early fruit of the international competition for export markets in the Third World which sprang up even before Europe and Japan had completely recovered from their wartime destruction. As early as 1950 an article in *Banking* noted that

> One of the reasons . . . the Administration favoured the Eximbank loan to Argentina was to get American machinery to the Rio Plate ahead of German machinery, for the sake of the replacement and reorder business to follow. *Washington wants to get Germany off the US taxpayer's back, but not at the expense of the US exporter*. Can we eat our cake and have it too?[87]

During the early 1950s, 'aid' was extended primarily to US dependencies in Asia and to Greece and Turkey, who were military allies of the United States. Defining 'foreign aid' is difficult since it has been extended in so many diverse forms: military credits, agricultural surplus disposal, disaster relief, etc. But there is general agreement among specialists that 'aid' is money or goods extended either without the requirement for repayment or with repayment terms that are measurably 'softer' than what would be demanded in the marketplace. ('Softer' terms mean that interest rates are lower, or grace periods and repayment schedules longer, than private creditors would allow.) The difference between the terms of 'aid' and commercial loan terms is a subsidy paid by taxpayers.

Thus 'aid' is one part of so-called capital flows,[88] but not all capital flows are aid. Two annual publications of the Organisation for Economic Cooperation and Development (OECD), *Financing and External Debt of Developing Countries* and *Development Cooperation*, break down total financial flows into several categories, which will give some idea of the complexity of the terminology.[89]

The 1950s also witnessed the first postwar Third World debt crises. Argentina in 1956, and Turkey in 1959, required multilateral debt rescheduling exercises, a technique which was novel at the time but soon became routinised.

9. Aid and the Cold War

The 1950s began with the triumph of the Red Army in China, the outbreak of the Korean War and the polarisation of military forces in Asia along Cold War lines, as China and North Korea sought help from the Soviet Union and the United States rushed military aid and economic aid (termed 'defence support') to Taiwan and South Korea. The origins of the US 'foreign aid' program lie in this military situation and in the Point Four program announced by President Harry Truman.

At that time it was not US policy to make official loans for economic development. The Point Four program, announced in 1949, emphasised technical assistance, or the transfer of knowledge. When Latin Americans requested 'Marshall Plan' aid, they were rebuffed by Secretary Marshall himself, who informed an Inter-American conference at Bogota, Colombia, that their path to development lay through 'individual effort and the use of private resources'.[90]

It was assumed that private investment would move the capital needed, while money flowed as military aid and defence support only to those governments willing to align themselves unambiguously with the United States against the Communist bloc. Congress authorised economic assistance with the idea that it would be phased out after two years, and as late as 1956 it 'seemed to be on the way out'.[91]

Secretary of State John Foster Dulles, however, felt the need for more. Walt Whitman Rostow, reminiscing on the origins of the Development Loan Fund, writes that Dulles

> said that . . . he was being forced to defend the interests of the United States with one arm tied behind his back; namely, the nation's economic strength. US military power – the other arm – was not enough and was, indeed, largely unusable.[92]

A group of former OSS[93] and CIA people turned academics, based in the CIA sponsored and funded Center for International Affairs at the Massachusetts Institute of Technology (CENIS), responded to Dulles' call to devise a 'World Economic Plan', an abortive first attempt at what would eventually become the Development Loan Fund. CENIS was the outgrowth of

'Project Troy', a psychological warfare project in which the CIA sought academic assistance from MIT. Max Millikan, previously of the CIA, was director of CENIS. Rostow would later occupy a high State Department position during the Vietnam War.

CENIS chose to present the 'positive side of the psychological warfare theme'.[94] Millikan and Rostow believed with Dulles that the great economic strength of the United States was its greatest asset. They held that 'to accomplish *its basically political and psychological purpose*, development assistance should be freed from purposes other than development.'[95]

The two published a book in 1957[96] that was primarily concerned with the communist 'threat' to the Third World. Military repression of local uprisings – counter-insurgency – was one prong of the proposed defence against this threat. But economic competition with the Soviet bloc demanded another complementary approach: large loans, which would be at least nominally devoted to economic development.

Although Millikan and Rostow may have been sincerely concerned with the need of poor countries for capital, they did not hesitate to use the purported needs of the *rich* countries to sell their proposal:

> [The industrialized countries] need two things: expanding markets in which they can sell those goods they can produce most cheaply, and expanding sources of food and raw materials . . . *Without a restoration of international trade there is little hope for finding a solution for the growth problems of the developed countries of Western Europe and Japan.*[97]
> In the short run the process of development itself generates requirements for capital goods and equipment which can provide an important outlet for European and Japanese manufacturers.[98]
> Fears that as they develop they will become competitors of presently industrialized countries and thus reduce export opportunities should be quieted by the history of industrialization.[99]

The *repayment* of loans (or divestment of foreign-owned assets) was not considered by Millikan and Rostow. They did, however, contemplate that after a given period of time a country would be able to finance its own investment without further net foreign borrowing. A rather vague illustration, based on what they admitted were arbitrary assumptions, concluded that a country could dispense with net borrowing after fourteen years:

> For example, if the initial rate of domestic investment in a country is 5 per cent of national income, if foreign capital is supplied at a constant rate equal to one-third the initial level of domestic investment, if 25 per cent of all additions to income are saved and reinvested, if the capital–output ratio is 3 and if interest and dividend service on foreign loans and private investment are paid at the rate of 6 per cent per year, the country will be able to discontinue net foreign borrowing after fourteen years and sustain a 3 per cent rate of growth out of its own resources.[100]

A few years later Millikan published, with another co-author, another book which illustrates just how closely the foreign aid program, firmly launched by then, was wedded to Cold War goals, and that it was frankly viewed as a bribe.

> It is in the interest of the United States to see emerging from the transition process nations with certain characteristics. First, they must be able to maintain their independence, especially of powers hostile or potentially hostile to the United States . . . Fourth, they must accept the principle of an open society whose members are encouraged to exchange ideas, goods, values, and experiences with the rest of the world; this implies as well that their governments must be willing to cooperate in the measures of international economic, political and social control necessary to the functioning of an interdependent world community.[101]
>
> For capital assistance to have the maximum leverage in persuading the underdeveloped countries to follow a course consistent with American and free-world interests . . . the amounts offered must be large enough and the terms flexible enough to persuade the recipient that the game is worth the effort. This means that we must invest substantially larger resources in our economic development programs than we have done in our past.[102]

The intellectual parents of postwar foreign economic aid were primarily cold warriors, and their economics was subservient to their political and psychological warfare aims. They were economists enough, however, to begin constructing theoretical castles based on nothing but airy counterfactual assumptions which would later be accepted as gospel truth by students of their profession. And on the repayment problem they sounded like Scarlett O'Hara: We'll think about that tomorrow, or maybe in twenty or thirty years.

10. Grants versus loans

> I think we are fooling ourselves and the world if we think that these loans are really going to be repaid. Indeed the soft loans (namely, the loans repayable in the currency of the borrowing country) tend in the very nature of the case to become disguised grants. We have had experience with that sort of thing before. Witness the First World War loans. The whole thing simply became unworkable . . . *Still, if grants are politically impossible, loans are far better than nothing. The problems of repayment will have to be dealt with in the future.*[103]

'[E]conomic development is hereafter made through loans and not through grants.'[104]

The implication, if one agreed with the author of the second quotation, was surely that if loans are better than nothing, worried economists should not be too frank in warning of the ultimate unrepayability of loans – for that might diminish the willingness of Congress to appropriate the money.

In the formative years of the US foreign loan program, the mid and late 1950s, the question of grants v. loans was discussed in the State Department and in Congress. The pro-aid faction within the administration faced stiff opposition to its proposals to establish an ongoing, semipermanent aid program, as contrasted with the previous *ad hoc* efforts. Two authors of a State Department memo on the subject in 1956, according to a historian's account,

> saw no real difference between grants and soft loans in terms of their economic effects. But they did note that some elements in Congress and the US public felt that soft loans [defined at that time as loans repayable in the currencies of the borrowers] were preferable to grants, and some recipients considered them less degrading. They suggested therefore that there were sound political reasons for shifting an increasing portion of aid to soft loans.[105]

The sentiments of Congress on this issue were typified by the remarks of Congressman John Vorys, who had suggested in 1954 that loans were preferable to grants:

> First, a person asking for a loan tries to make his proposition as good as possible, but a person asking for a grant tries to make it look as bad as possible. Second, a person asking for a loan knows that he *might* have to repay it, and therefore asks for as little as possible, whereas someone asking for a grant asks for as much as possible.[106]

The 'might' in this statement is revealing. No banker would make a loan which he thought the borrower *might* have to repay, but this seemed to be the sentiment of Congress. 'No one had definite views concerning repayment formulas,' according to one account of the establishment of the first program for lending to the Third World. John Foster Dulles remembered that Great Britain had to use credit from its colony India in wartime, and thought it would be useful to have some IOUs in the drawer in case the US should ever find itself in the position of debtor. 'No one at the State Department at that time took an interest in Dulles' statement, even though he encouraged research on the problem.'[107]

Since the aid program was originally set up by those who wished to wage a propaganda war against communism and those (such as US farmers) who wished to export their surpluses on credit, repayment was not a high priority item; indeed, as we will recall from Chapter 4, *supra*, on the transfer problem, repayment was held to be positively undesirable from the macroeconomic standpoint of the creditor country. The United States accumulated local or 'soft' currencies received in repayment of these loans, in 'counterpart' funds. On some occasions when the amounts of money in these funds became so high that the country in question began to feel uncomfortable about the potential threat to their economy if the United States ever decided to spend them, the United States would 'donate' the currencies back to the borrowing country, in well-publicised ceremonies. In 1961 the definition of 'soft' loans was changed, from local-currency repayment to hard currency repayment on easy terms.

It was assumed that the debtors also knew that loans did not have to be repaid. 'In a truly sanction-free bilateral situation, loans *are* grants if a candid creditor lets the expected net capital flow get below zero.' In other words, as soon as a debt relationship reaches the point of negative net transfer, the debtor will default if no other punishment is expected. Ironically (because the message was not taken to heart), the journal in which this comment appeared (in 1965) was published by the office of the US Comptroller of the Currency, one of the agencies responsible for overseeing the soundness of the US banking system.[108]

And yet, default or forgiveness of debt were not considered admissible options either. The amounts which some countries were obligated to pay in debt service were already considerable in 1960, only a few years after the establishment of the Development Loan Fund.

The problem was so serious that the World Bank published a book that year entitled *Debt Servicing Problems of Low-Income Countries 1956–58*. The authors of that book warned:

> . . . [I]n several major debtor countries, most of which already have high

debt service ratios, service payments are predicted to rise in the next few years.[109]

... [I]n some cases uncertain export prospects and heavy debt service schedules constitute a serious obstacle to substantial amounts of further borrowing.[110]

The preferred solution became rescheduling, combined with new lending. In debt rescheduling exercises, which will be described in more detail in Chapter 12, a given debtor country's major governmental creditors would meet in a forum which became known as the 'Paris Club' and negotiate a postponement of debt service obligations to future years. These rescheduling meetings were often closely associated with 'aid clubs' in which the same creditors would agree on the levels of aid, usually in the form of new loans, which they would provide in the next few years. In this form the option of 'lending in perpetuity' or lending the debtor the money with which to pay interest on its debts, was officially sanctioned. It is the model which is still used today.

Between 1957 and 1969 eleven debtor countries carried out a total of 21 debt-rescheduling exercises. (Argentina had four; Turkey, Ghana and Indonesia three each, and Brazil had two.) By deferring some debt service payments to later years, these reschedulings helped to postpone the approach of the 'break-even' point. And the creditor governments which granted the reschedulings, by insisting on IMF stand-by agreements as a condition of rescheduling, succeeded in fooling themselves and a number of private lenders and investors that the debtor nation's economic management had turned around sufficiently to justify new inflows of capital. This was even more important than reschedulings to the goal of avoiding the 'break-even' point.

The rescheduling of old debt and the inflow of new funds preserved for a time the net transfers, and the import surpluses, they financed, but at the price of a loss of respect for the integrity of the loan contract. As one expert noted,

Liberal and continual renegotiation or rescheduling of debt may undermine the legal and institutional framework which ensures that payments on international debt are treated as serious contractual obligations and which encourages the flow of capital from the rich countries to the poor. By penalizing the successful countries and rewarding those who fail to meet the service obligations, the incentive for good performance is weakened.[111]

There is an astounding sentence in an official publication of the International Monetary Fund, the organisation charged with telling debtor countries how to balance their foreign accounts:

[A]id to developing countries constitutes a continuous source of financing ... therefore the recipients are not expected to adjust their balance of payments to do without the aid as were the European countries during the immediate postwar period.[112]

The debtor countries noted this paradox and drew the conclusion they wished to draw (which was also, in a macroeconomic sense, correct): the creditor governments did not expect them to repay debts with their own money, and in fact did not want them to.

11. The Alliance for Progress

The decade of the 1950s ended with the triumph of Fidel Castro in Cuba, just as the previous decade had ended with the triumph of communism in China. Alarmed by the attraction which the Cuban revolution held for the disaffected classes in other countries in Latin America, US foreign policy towards that region was overhauled to make the capitalist model appear more attractive.

The Alliance for Progress, a brainchild of President Kennedy and his 'best and brightest' advisers, was hailed as the dawn of a new, enlightened era of US relations with Latin America. Large flows of aid finance were supposed to encourage and complement social measures such as land reform in order to raise standards of living and promote democratisation on the continent.

Yet the program was quickly detoured into a prop for governments which were willing to defend the interests of private foreign investors (mostly US corporations). The democratic and social reform hopes originally vested in it were quickly buried. And most of the gross flows of capital to Latin America during the decade served merely to replace the outflow due to profit remittances, and interest on public indebtedness, which had already mounted to $10 billion in 1960.

Two historians of the Alliance for Progress estimated that the grand total of economic assistance from the United States, international organisations, other developed countries and private aid was $18 billion in the years 1961–9. On a *net transfer* basis (gross disbursements less repayments and interest), however, the Latin American countries participating in the Alliance for Progress received only $4.8 billion from the United States from all sources.[113]

> If one further deducts the flow of profit remittance back to US private investors, 'that flow is about nil.'[114]

Thus the gross inflows of US and other foreign assistance merely compensated for the capital that was taken *out* of Latin America in the 1960s. But without this foreign assistance, '*a debt burden which existed at the beginning of the Alliance period in Latin American countries would have led to national bankruptcies* accompanied by severe reductions in production and amortization.'[115]

The editor of an economic journal on Latin America protested in pungent language against what he considered a hijacking of limited Alliance for Progress funds to provide 'retroactive insurance for careless creditors' unwilling to accept the consequences of their own imprudent lending.

> [T]o divert funds to retroactive insurance for European creditors means that much less for effective social progress activity. So that the well-being of Latin America is directly involved.[116]

In his view, a moratorium was the proper response to a debt crisis, and by far the best choice so far as the well-being of Latin America was concerned.

> [A]ny misuse of Alliance money, any diversion of such money from the economic and social purposes for which it was appropriated, works against the interest of Latin America. A moratorium involving ultimately a scaledown of principal consistent with the conditions alleged to exist in the debtor country could then have been followed by a fruitful use of the same amount of donations to the benefit of Latin America. Instead, under the misconception that they were in effect gypping the U.S. taxpayer, rather than hurting themselves, the Latins in effect underwrote their affluent creditors to their own lasting disadvantage.[117]

The same journalist condemned what he claimed was the diversion of more than a billion dollars of Alliance funds to the illegitimate purpose of compensating foreign investors for the nationalisation of no-longer-profitable investments.

> It remained, however, for a half-dozen corporations to top this performance in irresponsibility in an exercise of Secretary Rusk's self-defined 'dollar diplomacy modern-style' arranged with the full cooperation of U.S. officials and with the ignorant enthusiasm of their Latin American counterparts. During the [first] four years of the Alliance, arrangements were made to unload more than a billion dollars worth of direct investments on Latin American governments. More than half this amount involved properties that had once milked Latin American exchange resources impressively, but which had become steadily less profitable until they represented very minor drains on balance of payments for profit remittance.[118]

Significantly, one of the uses for the first international bank loans which were extended to Latin American governments in the late 1960s was to finance the 'nationalisation with compensation' of more foreign-owned investment properties. The theory was that the country would be better off paying interest on a loan than in allowing profit remittances without end, but it may be that the country got the short end of the deal.

Outside Latin America, new aid served to bail out old loans in all the heavily indebted countries. An IMF standby credit to the Philippines in 1970 was explicitly designed to help 'meet foreign debt obligations'. The World Bank urged the country's governmental creditors gathered in the Paris Club to effect a 'quick disbursement . . . on as liberal terms as possible'.

> Stated more directly the recommendation was tantamount to asking the governments to provide import finance on easy terms, so as to release Philippine earnings for payment of the debt owed to their banking institutions.[119]

The global picture was not very different. During the period 1964–7, the industrialised countries (organised for statistical purposes as the Development Assistance Committee of OECD) received an annual average of $3.7 billion of repatriated direct investment income from the so-called 'developing' countries. During the same period new direct investment averaged less than $1.3 billion a year, leaving a net drain on developing country resources of an average $2.4 billion yearly.[120]

Thus the Ponzi scheme was already at full gallop in the 1960s. New money lent merely sufficed to ensure that older debt was repaid. Even so, it had to be supplemented with debt reschedulings.

12. The Paris Club, the IMF and rescheduling

The first postwar reschedulings of Third World debt occurred in the late 1950s. Between 1956 and 1972 Argentina, Brazil, Cambodia, Chile, Ghana, India, Indonesia, Pakistan, Peru and Turkey[121] all came to what was called the 'Paris Club' (or its functional equivalent) in order to stretch out payments on a debt service burden, owed to government creditors, which had reached 'crisis' proportions. (The Paris Club is not a club at all but a set of procedures facilitated by the French Treasury, which provides meeting rooms and a secretariat.)

Imminent default, we are told by the author of one of the rare studies of the Paris Club, is one of three firm principles of the Club along with conditionality and burden sharing. The refusal to grant debt relief unless the country is in immediate danger of default is a necessary defence erected by creditors against capricious requests for debt relief.

> Creditor governments wil not entertain a request for debt relief unless there is evidence that the debtor country will default on its external payments in the absence of such relief. The existence of substantial external payment arrears is generally regarded as sufficient evidence that the imminent-default criterion has been met.[122]

This is too disingenuous, however. In practice, the creditors were almost always in control of the timing of a 'default' and could provoke it simply by deciding to withhold credit. In the circumstances of the 1956–72 period, the 'imminent default' situation was typically provoked by the creditors who desired to force a change in economic policies, and thus political choices, they disapproved and were no longer willing to finance.

In fact, as our source on the Paris Club later admits, 'rescheduling is usually triggered not when the debtor country submits a formal request for negotiations in the Paris Club but when the official creditors decide they are unwilling to continue extending credit to the debtor country.'[123]

The policy changes desired by creditors could come in one of two ways. The offending government of the debtor might be overthrown by a military coup. Scholars are still debating the extent of direct foreign (i.e. US CIA) support for such coups in Indonesia, Brazil, Chile and other countries in this group, but in any case no one doubted that plotters who captured a government and changed its policies to those favoured by creditor governments would receive a friendly reception when they asked for debt rescheduling and a renewal of aid.

Alternatively, a debt crisis could be provoked which would provide the creditors with the opportunity and the excuse to force on a government continuing in office the desired change in policies, by forcing the debtor to negotiate with the Paris Club and accept conditionality designed by the IMF before credit was resumed.

Once the debtor government had come, willingly or not, to the negotiating table, rescheduling had to be negotiated by all the creditors in concert because of the concern for 'burden sharing'. This is a variation of the 'bail-out' problem. The esence of the burden-sharing problem is that if one creditor, acting alone, decides to reschedule, reduce, or write off what it is owed by a problem debtor, its gesture will not benefit the debtor that still has to pay more money than it has to other creditors. Rather the debt reduction will benefit only the other, hard-line creditors because the money not needed to pay the generous creditor will simply be reallocated to service claims of the hardliners. The only solution to this problem was to get all the creditors into a room together and hammer out an agreement that would be applicable to all of them.

An interesting variation on the burden-sharing problem could be seen in cases like that of Indonesia after the ouster of Sukarno in 1966. The *old* foreign debt of Indonesia was owed predominantly to Soviet-bloc creditors, while the new pro-Western orientation of the country's military government meant they expected new aid from the West, which was in fact eager to support them. The Western creditors wanted to uphold the sanctity of debt obligations while at the same time they emphatically did not want to 'bail out' the Soviet bloc countries, which would have been the result of providing new aid or rescheduling debts to themselves while obligations to the Eastern creditors continued to be paid in full.

The solution was for the Western creditors to meet, although they held less than half of Indonesia's total debt, and negotiate drastic reductions (more generous than those given to any other debtor in this period) on condition that Indonesia would also seek the same reduction from its Eastern creditors. In essence, the Western creditors met and decided to forgive Indonesia's debt to the Soviet bloc. The Soviets, who did not intend to give aid to the new pro-Western government of Indonesia, acquiesced in the arrangement because without the carrot of future credit it was powerless to enforce collection of the old debt.

> The technique by which Paris Club creditors achieve burden sharing with nonparticipating official creditors is to include a 'nondiscrimination' clause in the standard rescheduling agreement. This clause commits the debtor country to obtaining equivalent debt relief from all its nonparticipating official creditors. If it accepts harder terms from any of them, then it is obligated to repay the Paris Club creditors more rapidly.[124]

The third principle of the Paris Club, conditionality, was the most controversial and had the most damaging long-term effects on the development of future debt crises. Each debtor was required, as a condition of debt rescheduling, to negotiate a 'stand-by agreement' (a kind of international line of credit) with the International Monetary Fund, an agreement which was made conditional on the adoption of an austerity, or stabilisation, program with the professed purpose of reducing domestic consumption, increasing export capabilities and thereby enabling nations to turn their finances around and service their debts.

It was only to be expected that creditors would be unwilling to continue financing what they considered to be profligate behaviour on the part of debtors; it is by no means illegitimate for creditors to seek guarantees of good economic behaviour and indications of future solvency from those who wish to borrow from them.

The problem lay, rather, in the nature of the conditions which were required (and still are, for little has changed in the subsequent years) as part of the stabilisation program, for, regarded critically, these conditions were exactly the wrong ones for a country trying to reduce its foreign debts. The regressive social and political consequences of IMF austerity programs have been criticised at exhaustive length elsewhere.[125] Our concern here is with how these reschedulings fit into the overall Ponzi scheme of Third World debt.

If one is primarily concerned with enabling a country to pay back its debts and prevent future debt crises, some of the IMF conditions would be unobjectionable. Devaluation, for example, despite some unfortunate distributive consequences, should provide incentives for conserving foreign exchange and stimulate local production both for domestic consumption and for export. Balanced budgets are laudable even if there are bitter disputes about who should be taxed and which government programs should be cut in order to achieve the balance.

But other, more fundamental objectives of the stabilisation program were destined to frustrate and doom the potential good effects of such measures. Specifically, the combination of import and exchange liberalisation measures and the rescheduling and new credit which were provided as incentives for their adoption inevitably *worsened* the debtor's balance of payments and debt problems over the long run and virtually guaranteed that there would be newer and larger debt crises in the future.

Import and exchange controls were designed to conserve scarce foreign exchange, which is highly desirable in a crisis. Yet the key demand of the IMF (which was only the collective voice of the creditor countries) was the abolition or loosening of such controls. Liberalisation of controls meant that the power of budgeting this scarce resource for the most necessary and socially desirable uses was not available to the debtor. Even though such budgeting should not have been used in lieu of other necessary reforms, abolishing the very possibility of budgeting and conservation of foreign exchange was exactly the wrong thing to do.

The arguments used by the IMF in favour of this counter-intuitive 'reform' were those used later by the Reagan administration and its cohorts in the United States, i.e. that the market is the only efficient allocator of scarce resources. But although repeatedly touting the virtues of the market, the IMF itself was not a market mechanism at all, and the collective activities of the creditor governments, both in their separate capacities as aid givers and loan guarantors and through their collective alter ego, the IMF, tended to frustrate whatever good market forces, such as devaluation, might have otherwise been able to effect.

The chief non-market intervention committed by the creditors was the supply of new loans to debtors already struggling under heavy future obligations which had been merely stretched out, not forgiven, under most of the rescheduling arrangements. This is not done in the Paris Club negotiations, but separately by the same creditor governments; while there is a formal separation of the debt forgiveness and new credit functions, they are in practice closely linked.

These flows of funds were decidedly not driven by market forces, and they were sizeable enough to distort the supposed 'market' incentives praised by the IMF. While devaluation theoretically discouraged imports, new credit encouraged them by financing the inflow of goods and services the creditors wished to sell, no longer hindered by import controls. 'Capital flight' was perfectly legal under liberalised exchange regimes. The availability of foreign aid to fill a 'financing gap' calculated by the IMF was a powerful incentive *not* to achieve a balanced budget, since without a deficit a country would *appear* to have no need for new aid or credits.

There was, as our source on the Paris Club admits,

> a large contradiction at the heart of the Paris Club process. Creditors should reward far-reaching measures that lead to a rapid restoration of creditworthiness by offering more generous terms. Yet the stronger the corrective measures taken by a debtor country, the less relief is needed. Thus, creditors cannot reward good policies without violating the first principle. They cannot give relief that is not needed.[126]

The net effect of the IMF-designed stabilisation programs was to 'bail out' the debtors from their immediate crisis, provoked, as explained above, by the creditors themselves, while piling up obligations for the future. In nearly every case, the sum of the old, pre-crisis debts was quickly dwarfed by the massive sums of new, post-crisis loans. It was not just the worst conceivable way to solve a debt crisis, it was a short-term palliative which made the situation worse. It was, on the other hand, a very effective means to allow creditors to continue to sell goods to the debtor while exerting foreign control over the debtor's economy; and thus a telling indicator of the real agenda of the creditor governments. Good performance in meeting rescheduled debts was not valued as highly as faithful submission to IMF demands which actually worsened future debt service capabilities.[127]

The real beneficiaries of 'liberalisation' were the exporters of the creditor countries who were thus able to continue to sell their goods, financed by credit from their own or other creditor governments. At the same time they exerted control over the debtor which would have been called imperialistic if exercised by only one country, rather than by the creditors' cartel.

13. The crisis of 1970

The system was inherently unstable, and it was already in crisis by the end of the 1960s, a condition amply documented in a flurry of reports produced by blue-ribbon commissions around 1970. The appointment of the Pearson commission in 1968 by Robert McNamara, incoming president of the World Bank, was part of the attempt by American leaders to deal with that crisis.

Partners in Development, the report of the Pearson commission published in 1969, predicted that debt service burdens would mount to the point of crisis in the next decade. The percentage of gross new lending eaten up by debt service in 1965–7 had reached 87 per cent in Latin America. The net transfer would become *negative* before 1977 for most areas of the Third World unless gross flows were radically accelerated (or debt service sharply reduced) in the early 1970s. The Pearson commission calculations indicated that even if gross flows rose by 8 per cent per annum, debt service would consume between 60 and 89 per cent of gross lending by 1977.

Table 13.1
Debt Service as Percentage of Gross Lending
(as projected by Pearson Commission in 1969)

	Africa	*Europe*	*East Asia*	*South Asia and Middle East*	*Latin America*
1965–7	73	92	52	40	87
1977					
Variant A: gross flow of new lending unchanged	121	109	134	97	130
Variant B: new lending increases by 8 per cent per annum	77	71	88	60	89

Source: Report of the Commission on International Development, *Partners in Development*, Lester B. Pearson, chairman (New York and London: Praeger, 1969) p. 74.

Other debt experts were similarly pessimistic. One concluded that in order to keep *net* levels of assistance constant over the decade of the 1970s, gross lending would have to increase 200 per cent, or 12 per cent per annum. Further, he concurred with the Pearson commission conclusion that it was imperative for the net flows to be made on soft terms.

> Any attempt to finance large capital flows to an average LDC over a period of 10 to 20 years, except on soft terms, results in debt service payments which soon threaten to become unmanageable.[128]

Another expert warned, 'In the face of persistent balance of payments deficits, the strain has been increasing to the extent that the situation has sometimes been described as the "debt explosion".'[129] The problem was aired in the business press: 'Latin governments seeking to refinance their heavy foreign debt burdens will run into some reluctance in international banking circles. . . . The terms demanded for such refinancing will no doubt be raised.'[130]

Nelson Rockefeller reported to the US President on the problems of Latin America in 1969:

> Heavy borrowing by some Western hemisphere countries to support development have reached the point where annual repayments of interest and amortization absorb a large share of foreign exchange earnings. . . . Many of the countries are, in effect, having to make new loans to get the foreign exchange to pay interest and amortization on old loans, and at higher interest rates.

The report recommended 'a generous rescheduling of debt service requirements for countries facing balance of payments problems'.[131]

Nelson's brother David Rockefeller was chairman of Chase Manhattan Bank, one of the US money centre banks which was shortly to embark on the Third World lending craze. David Rockefeller, who surely was familiar with his brother's conclusions, also sat on another Task Force on International Development. The Peterson commission, chaired by Rudolph Peterson, then president of Bank of America (another present and future lender to the Third World), had the assignment of recommending a new approach to US foreign aid for the 1970s. It said of the debt burden of 1970:

> The debt burden of many developing countries is now an urgent problem. It was foreseen, but not faced, a decade ago. It stems from a combination of causes [but] whatever the causes, future export earnings of some countries are so heavily mortgaged as to endanger continuing imports, investment, and development.[132]

Among other recommendations, the report proposed that the government *guarantee* foreign official borrowing on international capital markets as a transitional device to help countries become independent of US concessional lending.[133] Rockefeller's and Peterson's banks stood to make a mint of money, of course, on lending to the Third World, and a government guarantee would have made that profit risk-free.

Mexico was one country caught in the shrinking net transfer. Of $724 million in loans contracted in 1971, $455 million was earmarked for amortisation of old debt and $235 million for interest payments. This left a mere $31 million – a scant 4 per cent of the gross lending – for 'investment'.[134]

Robert McNamara issued his own sombre warning in a 1972 speech:

> Since the mid-1950s, publicly guaranteed debt has been growing at about 14% a year. At the end of 1971 it stood at over $60 billion and annual debt service exceeded $5 billion. Servicing of debt since the mid-1950s has been growing at the same annual average rate of about 14%. This is about twice the rate at which the export earnings, from which the debt must be serviced, have been growing. *Such a relationship cannot continue indefinitely.*[135]

The United Nations Conference on Trade and Development convened an *ad hoc* group of governmental experts on debt problems of developing countries in 1974. The Organisation of Economic Cooperation and Development produced its own report on the subject in the same year. The US Congress held hearings inquiring into the failure to collect debts owed to the United States by various Third World countries.

One reason for the rapid escalation in debt service was the hardening of terms for so-called 'aid'. Suppliers' and other commercial credits had always been extended on market terms, but, in the beginning, foreign aid had been largely in grant form. But as we have seen, by the end of the 1950s the US Congress was getting tired of 'giveaways' and insisted increasingly on the use of loans rather than grants. Lester Pearson, the chairman of the Pearson commission, explained in his own 1969 book, *The Crisis of Development*, that

> the proportion of loans to grants-in-aid flows has gone up from 13 per cent to 50 per cent in the last ten years. In addition, the terms of official loans have hardened, from an average rate of 3.1 per cent in 1964 to 3.3 per cent in 1968. World Bank loans, which were as low as 4.5 per cent in the late 1940s, reached seven per cent in that year. Loan maturities were down from 28.4 years to 24.8 years.[136]

But as we have seen, in the earlier years serious thinkers did not seriously expect *or want* these debtors to repay their debts – at least not in a net sense. The collective amnesia about this assumption was one of the first signs of the danger which ultimately led to the credit collapse. In the following decade, all restraints would dissolve in an orgy of lending to countries whose creditworthiness, in fact nonexistent, would be loudly endorsed by precisely those in the best position to know better.

14. Don't blame OPEC

As we saw in previous chapters, several major Third World nations had suffered debt crises in the 1960s and by 1970 the Third World as a whole was approaching the 'break-even' point at which debt service exceeded new capital inflows. It was no secret that the best-informed people in the field expected many debtor countries to default when they reached this break-even point, and that prevailing attitudes on the 'necessity' of capital inflows and the practice of debt rescheduling might encourage the borrowers to do just that. It is deeply ironic, then, that it should have been precisely at this moment that commercial bankers chose to abandon their long-held scepticism on the safety of international lending and began to throw hundreds of billions of dollars at Third World countries already deeply in debt. One of the biggest mysteries of the whole saga is the question: Why did they do it?

We must first deal with the prevailing myth. It is commonly believed that commercial bank lending to the Third World was a response to the four-fold increase in the price of crude petroleum which member countries of OPEC announced in 1973–4.

There are two versions of this explanation. One holds that the higher price of oil was a severe blow to oil importing Third World countries, and the banks, in the spirit of public service, recycled the money in order to allow these countries to import and pay for the petroleum their economies desperately needed.

This version has some truth in the case of two major debtors, Brazil and South Korea. Both are dependent on imported oil and both did increase their international borrowing after the 'oil shock', rather than cut back on investment programs. (It is also true of several small countries such as Jamaica.)

The energy crisis was not, however, a serious problem for other Latin American nations; most, except for Brazil and Central America, were either net exporters of oil or largely self-sufficient in energy. Further, the prices of *their* export commodities were at record high levels, so on balance they were benefited rather than harmed by the commodity price boom.[137]

Most bank lending did *not* go to the countries damaged by the higher price of oil. Some of these countries, such as Bangladesh, actually remained net *creditors* of the international banks throughout the period of oil price rises.

It was the oil *exporting* countries such as Indonesia, Venezuela, Algeria,

Nigeria and Mexico that got the lion's share of the new commercial credit. Indeed, IMF statistics show that net oil *exporters* (excluding the obvious Middle Eastern ones: Iraq, Iran, Kuwait, Libya, Oman, Qatar, Saudi Arabia and United Arab Emirates) borrowed significantly *more* relative to their export earnings and GNP than the net oil importers.

Table 14.1
Long-term and Short-term External Debt Relative to Exports and GNP 1977–84

	1977	*1978*	*1979*	*1980*	*1981*	*1982*	*1983*	*1984*
Ratio of external debt to exports of goods and services:								
Net oil exporters:	179.8	174.8	143.6	127.0	156.3	188.0	198.3	189.0
Net oil importers:	116.6	119.4	112.0	107.8	115.3	134.5	139.2	135.3
Ratio of external debt to GNP:								
Net oil exporters:	38.6	38.9	37.2	33.8	36.5	48.1	55.8	54.4
Net oil importers:	21.5	22.0	21.3	22.2	25.3	29.6	33.3	34.3

Source: IMF, *World Economic Outlook 1984*, Table 36.

The second variety of 'oil-shock' explanation for the bank lending boom focuses on the lending banks rather than the borrowing countries. According to this version, as dollars accumulated in the hands of governments of oil exporting countries, with Saudi Arabia and Kuwait at the pinnacle, these countries stuffed their cash into accounts with the large international private banks, who were faced with the problem of finding profitable outlets for their money. Under this pressure, they began to lower their standards for creditworthy borrowers.

There is no question that the oil surplus countries did place large sums of money into the Western banking system. But at best this is only part of the explanation.

Dollars deposited by OPEC surplus countries such as Saudi Arabia and Kuwait were only a fraction of the total sums invested in the Eurodollar market (IMF experts estimate it was only about 15 per cent).[138] Third World loans were also made from banks located in the United States, who borrowed the money to fund those loans both from the Eurodollar market and from regional and small-town banks within the United States.

Third World lending from the international commercial banks was likewise only a fraction (albeit a much larger one) of the total lending of these banks.

It can also be argued that the OPEC price rises which put money into the hands of oil producers took that money out of the hands of oil *purchasers* who would otherwise have deposited comparable sums in the banking system. In other words, the major change caused by the OPEC price rise was redistributing the funds to accounts held by oil exporting countries or their citizens, rather than an increase in the total amount of money in the banking system. The total number of dollars in the world does not change unless the emitting country, the United States in the case of the dollars, expands its emission.

The United States *did* expand its printing of dollars and there *was* a larger total amount of money in the banking system, but this *preceded* the oil price rise (and some say, encouraged it). Most of the major industrial countries simultaneously pumped up their money supply in the early 1970s, encouraged by the new 'floating exchange rate system' which seemed to promise that domestic inflation would result in no balance of payments cost.

> The explosion of money creation following Nixon's removal of the gold constraint produced an immense rise in *all* commodity prices in 1972–73 and the beginnings of the inflation that would wrack the democratic societies for a decade. When the oil producers began leapfrogging their prices, the money was there.[139]

But perhaps the most compelling evidence against the thesis that oil prices caused the lending boom to Third World countries is the timing of that lending. And here the official statistics collectors are emphatic: bank lending to Third World countries began *and experienced its greatest relative expansion* well *before* the oil price rise. The OECD itself made this clear:

> The most popular version of this [explanation for the rise in bank lending] associates it with the recycling of the oil surplus by private banks after 1973. In fact, it is absolutely clear . . . that *the most decisive and dramatic increase in bank lending to developing countries was associated with the major commodity price boom of 1972–73 – before the oil shock*, which struck in late 1973. From a 1971 figure of US $8 billion (at 1983 prices and exchange rates), bank lending expanded to more than US $18 billion in 1973, and as a share of total flows from 15 per cent in 1971 to 29 per cent in 1973. *Bank lending thereafter levelled off for the next two years, despite the enormous increase in oil bills.*[140]

A second surge of bank lending occurred between 1976 and 1978. Like the first, this second wave occurred in the context of liquidity creation and inflation in the United States, which contributed to another commodity price boom in the Third World. The second wave of lending preceded the second (1978–9) oil shock, after which bank lending again slowed.

Other sources confirm that the big expansion in lending preceded the oil price rise:

> For Mexico, the most important rise in contracted debt (before the stupendous borrowing of 1980) occurred between 1970 and 1974. Borrowing in 1973 was 200 per cent higher than in the previous year.[141]

The story is the same for Brazil, an oil importer: 'The turn to borrowing from foreign banks became clear by 1970 and pronounced by 1973.'[142] Nor was this timing peculiar to the countries named: they, and all the others, were borrowing because the banks were lending. 'In 1973, the market entered its first boom cycle, which is still regarded as the high point of indiscriminate lending in the 1970s. . . . No one had ever seen a borrower's market quite like this one.'[143] And yet the oil price rise was not announced until the *end* of 1973. We must seek the cause of the Third World lending boom elsewhere. We can't blame it on OPEC.

15. The World Bank and the debt problem

In order to understand why bank lending to the Third World became so important in the 1970s, it is necessary to return briefly to the 1960s and even earlier. The US government had tried ceaselessly since the end of World War II to draw private investors and lenders back into the financing of Third World deficits, against the private market's own self-preserving instincts born of the defaults of the 1930s. Succeeding administrations have never deviated from the view that the introduction of private capital investment into the Third World was the goal towards which they aimed, and a variety of means and of taxpayers' moneys was used to sweeten the deal for hesitant investors.

The functioning of the so-called 'free' market actually requires a heavy panoply of governmental involvement, subsidies and special organisations. The efforts of the US government included the subsidisation of US exports through guarantees by Eximbank and the Agency for International Development, which were continually expanded throughout the 1960s, and the creation of the Overseas Private Investment Corporation (OPIC) to provide public insurance against war, revolution, currency inconvertibility and other non-economic risks. The involvement of the multilateral World Bank is one of the most important and most interesting of these efforts.

The efforts began with the founding of the World Bank itself. According to the charter of the Bank, its purposes included:

> (i) To assist in . . . development . . . by facilitating the investment of capital for productive purposes, including . . . the encouragement of the development of productive facilities and resources in less developed countries.
>
> (ii) To promote private foreign investment by means of guarantees or participations in loans and other investments made by private investors. . . .
>
> (iii) To promote the long-range balanced growth of international trade and the maintenance of equilibrium in balances of payments by encouraging international investment for the development of the productive resources of members. . . .
>
> (v) To conduct its operations with due regard to the effect of international investment on business conditions. . . .[144]

The World Bank (and the developed industrial countries that determined its policies) devoted tremendous efforts to attempts to facilitate the eventual resumption of private credit flows to the Third World. The Bank, for example, insisted that Latin American countries to which it lent reach a mutually agreed settlement with the bondholders who had suffered from the defaults of the 1930s. 'Existing defaults are the most obvious obstacle to the restoration of credit,' according to the Bank's second annual report.[145]

The Bank also insisted that borrowing countries adopt policies which were calculated to attract private foreign capital. Such 'conditionality', which became a contentious issue in the 1970s and 1980s, was present in the very first loans made by the Bank to Latin American countries in the late 1940s.

While the US government was willing to extend military aid and economic aid designated as 'defence support' to its dependencies and military allies, it also assumed that for the business of ordinary economic development the government's function was to be a pump-primer for private capital.

The decade of the 1960s saw an intensification of efforts on the part of the governments of capital-exporting countries to introduce Third World borrowers to their private capital markets. The Agency for International Development began to guarantee high-risk bank loans to the Third World as early as 1962.[146] US Federal Reserve Guidelines called for 'the highest priority on bank loans to be given less developed countries in the granting of nonexport credits' and diplomatic posts were circularised to announce the fact – at a time, in 1965, when loans to other areas of the world were inhibited by US credit controls.[147]

The Eximbank and the Foreign Credit Insurance Corporation liberalised their rules the same year to allow increased export financing by commercial banks, including smaller ones.[148] The Fed amended its regulations again in 1967, making it easier for US banks to lend to and invest in the stock of foreign banks, and the Eximbank announced in 1969 that it would guarantee loans by *foreign* banks that finance US exports, because private US lenders were not meeting the demand.[149] A Congressional conference committee urged in 1971 that bank loans to finance US exports should be entirely excluded from the Fed's 'voluntary' ceilings on loans to foreign borrowers, and the Fed was happy to comply with the request.[150] President Nixon doubled the ceiling for Export–Import Bank programs at the same time.[151]

The World Bank, dominated by the United States and other creditor nations, held a special place as the official collector of foreign debt statistics. Its pronouncements on the debt question carried particular weight, as it was assumed to be privy to the best information on debt and debt service burdens. The annual reports of the World Bank for the 1960s revealed a striking pattern of double-think which was representative of the schizophrenia which dominated official thinking on debt.

On the one hand they documented and warned of the growing debt burden of Bank clients, while advocating softer terms for official finance:

> The heavy debt burden that weighs on an increasing number of its

member countries has been a continuing concern of the World Bank group . . . the Executive Directors have decided that the Bank itself may vary some terms of its lending to lighten the service burden in cases where this is appropriate . . . to the debt position of the country.[152]

[A]dequate supply [of] externally provided capital . . . is one of the most important [problems of development] . . . and its urgency has been greatly heightened by the increasing burden of debt servicing.[153]

While the increasingly heavy debt burden of developing countries points to the need for funds on easier terms . . . the average terms of total bilateral assistance may become less, rather than more, concessionary . . .

A higher level of aid on inappropriate terms, however, could make the external debt problem even more difficult. If aid is not made available on average terms which are more concessionary, the gross volume of assistance will have to be steeply and continuously increased in order to maintain any given level of real resources transfer.[154]

But at the same time the Bank's reports continued to advocate and cheer on increased lending from private capital markets, which would necessarily be on 'hard' or market terms.

The World Bank group and other international organizations . . . *are making strenuous efforts to encourage and enlarge the flow of private capital into the less developed countries.* There is no doubt that this flow can be expected to increase . . . thereby accelerating the pace of development and relieving the pressure on public funds.[155]

[I]t is to be hoped that conditions can be established in world [private] capital markets which will permit a freer movement of capital internationally.[156]

[After a long discussion of debt servicing difficulties]: None of this, however, should be taken to mean that developing countries cannot afford, and hence should avoid, any increases in debt service obligations.[157]

In 1957 the World Bank prepared a study at the request of UNCTAD on the problem of private suppliers' credits. These credits, which were extended by or on behalf of exporters wishing to sell goods to Third World countries, were, at that time, the heaviest part of the debt servicing burden for problem debtors, because they were lent on commercial terms, with high interest rates and short maturities. The share of payments on suppliers' credits as a percentage of total debt-service payments in 1965 was estimated to be 63 per cent for Brazil, 59 per cent for Argentina, 60 per cent for Nigeria, 49 per cent for Yugoslavia and 33 per cent for Turkey.

The staff study made several recommendations for dealing with the suppliers' credit problem, including the suggestion that only 'economically sound projects' should be financed and that better statistics on the problem be collected. The study also suggested:

> further consideration by creditor countries of arrangements to separate the financing and commercial aspects of the sale of capital goods, in particular *by placing greater emphasis on the use of financial rather than commercial credits.*[158]

In its *Annual Report* for 1971 the World Bank gave its most extensive and sombre analysis of the Third World debt crisis. (In the following years, which were precisely the years of the commercial bank lending boom, the debt problem was given only a cursory technical summary.) The 1971 report noted a 'phenomenal' growth in loans from private banks and other financial institutions, such as insurance companies and private investment syndicates. At the same time as this private lending on 'hard' terms was rapidly increasing, net flows from official sources on concessional terms was stagnant.

> The initiative for the supply of external finance thus appears to be shifting gradually from the public to the private sector, with clear implications for both the terms and the geographic distribution of global flows. . . . [D]ebt service owed to private creditors over the next few years is already very high in relation to private debt outstanding.[159]
>
> [Projection of capital flows over the next few years has been started by the Bank] and the initial results give little cause for optimism. . . . [L]ittle significant increase can be expected over the next decade in the net transfer figure of roughly $5 billion. . . .[I]t would appear inevitable that some individual developing countries would face the prospect of reduced growth rates or debt servicing difficulties.[160]

When the stock of debt outstanding at the end of 1969 was compared with debt service due in the following six years (1970–5), it was calculated that debt service due to private creditors was 84 per cent of total debt outstanding, and in some countries – Argentina, Brazil, Mexico, Peru, the Philippines and Yugoslavia – 100 per cent or more of the outstanding debt to private creditors would be due within the six years.[161] Unless stupendous sums of new lending became available, the reversal of the net transfer from positive to negative would be a certainty.

The stupendous sums did become available, but on hard commercial terms. Thus the 'disaster' of a negative net transfer was averted in the short term only to be postponed to the 1980s – and magnified enormously in scope.

16. Enter the banks

By the 1960s, a new generation of bankers who did not remember the lessons of the 1930s were taking control of their corporations. Enticed by the subsidies and guarantees offered by Eximbank and other government programs, and following their multinational customers who were expanding in the Third World (primarily Latin America) these banks rapidly developed a network of correspondent or branch banks in the countries they found most promising.

Under the guidance of the World Bank and its 'private sector' affiliate, the International Finance Company (IFC), they founded 'development finance companies' in several Third World countries in which they had business interests. These DFCs borrowed investment capital for foreign investors on local financial markets (thus causing critics of the multinationals to complain they did not even bring new money into the country). But more importantly, they also served as conduits for the distribution of foreign exchange borrowed from the parent banks and other lenders such as the World Bank and the IFC.[162]

The banks knew very well that some of the countries they did business in were experiencing debt crises. A senior vice-president of Citibank excoriated Argentina, Bolivia, Brazil, Chile, Uruguay and Colombia in 1965 as deadbeats which 'year after year have had to come back to Washington for bail-out loans and foreign debt stretch-outs.'[163] Years later the same man was a prominent defender of Citibank's loans to those same countries. *Business Latin America* reported that the average debt service ratio for Latin America was at least 14 per cent in 1966 and quoted the Inter-American Development Bank's even higher estimate, which included profit remittance in the numerator, of 20 per cent.[164]

As we saw in Chapter 13, Rudolph Peterson, former president of the Bank of America, and Nelson Rockefeller, brother of the chairman of Chase Manhattan, each chaired a commission which produced reports on the development and debt crises of Latin America in 1970. One suggestion made in the Peterson report was that the US government should smooth the access to international capital markets for the more 'creditworthy' borrowers in Latin America and elsewhere. Mexico, remarked *Business Latin America*, was already well on the way.[165]

Even before the oil shock focused general world attention on Third World borrowing, financial trade publications were speculating that the banks were *already* in over their heads. An editorial in the *Wall Street Journal* warned of imprudent Eurodollar loans early in 1971.[166]

'They're engaging in types of business and pricing practices that their head offices could never engage in at home,' a First National City Bank vice-president told a *Wall Street Journal* reporter, whose article was headlined 'Eager Lenders'.[167] Almost a year before the oil shock, an article headlined 'Uneasy Money' rephrased the same warning: 'a lot of banks are doing things internationally they wouldn't dream of doing domestically.'[168]

The journal of the American Bankers Association warned in 1969 that

> Many poor nations have already incurred debts past the possibility of repayment. . . . The US continues to make more loans to underdeveloped countries than any other country or organization and also has the greatest loss ratio, says a GAO report on AID. The trend toward making loans repayable in dollars does not ensure that the funds will be repaid.[169]
>
> International loans, even if made on 'businesslike' terms, have a way of getting lost unless they are repaid out the proceeds of additional loans.[170]

An official from Manufacturers Hanover (a bank that almost went bankrupt in the 1980s from its overexposure to Third World debt) was quoted in 1970 as worrying that banks were not paying enough attention to the creditworthiness of foreign borrowers.[171]

Why did the banks do it if (as we have seen) their senior executives knew very well the sorry debt record of many of their new clients? Anyone who read the newspapers (or the World Bank reports mentioned in the previous chapter) knew also that the prospects for increasing foreign aid (which had bailed out private-sector investors in the 1960s) was not good in the early 1970s. And yet, in the words of the *International Currency Review*, 'the entire international financial community . . . were collectively duped into accepting as normal, prudent banking practice, the inflation of the biggest bubble in the history of commercial banking.'[172]

Several partial answers may be suggested:

- Attractive borrowers were scarce in the usual bank markets, as many prime corporate borrowers began to bypass the banks and raise funds by issuing their own paper. The competition among banks for clients was fierce.
- Banks followed their corporate customers operating overseas. Those corporations were adopting a strategy of financing new projects by borrowing rather than by investing their own money. This strategy was a response to nationalism directed against multinational corporations which had arisen in Latin America and elsewhere in the late 1960s. Host countries, the corporations reasoned, could not expropriate loans. And, by mobilising several powerful Northern institutions, including the World Bank, in one financing package, the investors made it much more difficult for a nationalistic government to repudiate the debt without punishment from the world financial community.[173]

• The banks were enchanted with new techniques which seemed to minimise or hedge risks: 'floating-rate' loans which put the burden of interest-rate fluctuations on the borrowers, and syndicated credits, which gave dozens or even hundreds of different banks relatively modest participations in loans of enormous size.

• Lenders made easy profits from loans for huge sums which carried high 'spreads' (the difference between the bank's cost of borrowing the money on the interbank market and the interest paid by the non-bank borrowers) and fat 'front-end fees' (fees collected by the banks for organising the loans and deducted from the sums made available to the borrowers) but required relatively little executive time for appraisals and paperwork. Ironically, the spreads were high precisely because Third World borrowers, particularly sovereign borrowers, *were known to be bad risks*. The high profitability encouraged loan officers to forget the long-term risk; the short-term rewards were juicy and by the time troubles showed up everyone would have forgotten who was responsible. 'There appears to be no mechanism whatever for penalizing those who make bad loans on the grand scale . . . Walter Wriston remains chairman of Citibank . . . and his chief lending officers keep their loan commissions,' grumbled the editor of *International Currency Review* after the crisis broke.[174] Little time and attention were needed for appraisal of loan risk because, for reasons given below, the banks were making certain assumptions which allowed them to short-circuit the usual tedious processes.

• In several major debtor countries, the governments and/or policies which were blamed for previous debt crises had been changed. The military coups (Brazil 1964, Chile 1973, Argentina 1966 and 1976, Indonesia 1965–6, etc.), martial law declarations (Philippines 1972) and less obvious changes of economic policy by other governments allowed the banks to believe that the old, bad policies that produced previous defaults had been changed and that borrowing governments were now on the right track. Some of these coups, changes of policy and/or governing teams were provoked by cut-offs of external credit; many were supervised by the International Monetary Fund, which gave the banks a false sense that their loans were henceforth secure. Even where there was no current IMF agreement, the banks believed that any prospective crisis could be solved by bringing in the IMF whenever one threatened.

• The evaluation of risk was not an activity that was valued highly or rewarded in the go-go atmosphere of the late 1960s and early 1970s. 'The country information that was available within the money-center banks was flawed; even had it been "good" information, it would not have diverted the major money-center banks from a course largely directed by the pressures of excess liquidity and increased competition.'[175]

• When the banks did try to do some serious analysis of the long-term risks involved in their new lending, the unsophisticated tool of the 'debt service ratio' encouraged them to look chiefly at the export prospects of the borrowing countries. And the export prospects looked excellent, especially in the critical two years before the oil price explosion (and for oil exporters, even better *after* the oil price explosion). Commodity prices had risen to unprecedented highs, while the Club of Rome produced a widely publicised report claiming that the world was 'running out of resources'.[176] Unless one had long experience with the boom-and-bust volatility of raw materials prices (and the young lending officers seldom had such an experience) it was plausible to imagine that the producers of such commodities were going to be creditworthy in the future – even if they demonstrably had not been in the past.

A 1973 article by two IMF staff members on the new fad for bank lending to LDCs reported that 'the existence of natural resources is considered generally as sufficient evidence of credit worthiness.'[177] Another article by IMF staff eight years later reemphasised the procyclical nature of bank lending:

> Bank lending tended to move with the commodity price cycle. Although it would be difficult to regard this as simple cause and effect, the fact is that loan commitments soared during periods of price booms for minerals and primary commodity exports, but declined sharply – and in some cases dropped to almost nothing – when earnings from such exports fell.[178]

- The last point is the most important one, the supposed ace in the hole: the banks were assuming that bad debts could be made good just as they always had been in the recent past: with rescheduling and an infusion of new money from the interested governments of the creditor countries.

The banks did not fear rescheduling, as long as they could continue to collect market rates of interest; indeed, the first reschedulings of bank debt, in the late 1970s and early 1980s, made loans apparently even more profitable for the banks because they could increase the spreads and collect fat front-end fees for the rescheduling which were counted as instant profits.[179]

It is clear that in case of default, the banks expected to be saved by a government bail-out. These quotations from *Euromoney*, the trade publication of international banking, indicate their thinking in the mid-1970s:

> Though it was never articulated in so many words, most bankers must also have assumed that loans lent to LDC governments would be underwritten by the official aid programs of the developed world. No Western government had any wish to see a debtor country default, or to inflict a major loss on its own banking system.[180]
>
> On the one hand, a purely technical analysis of the [non-oil developing countries'] current financial position would suggest that defaults are inevitable; yet on the other hand, many experts feel this is not likely to happen. The World Bank, the IMF, and the governments of major industrialized nations, they argue, would step in rather than watch any default seriously disrupt the entire Euromarket apparatus.[181]
>
> In the case of such countries as South Korea, the Philippines, Taiwan or Israel, it is reasonable to expect that the day of default would be forestalled indefinitely as long as the stake of the US government in their economic and political stability remains high.[182]

One of the most tragic ironies of the decades-long debt drama was that the rise of raw materials prices did indeed hold the promise of allowing at least some countries to surmount their debt burden and to reduce it by repaying some principal. The enhanced prospects of commodity exporters should have meant that their need to borrow was *less* urgent. They had the opportunity to pay off their debt burdens from the 1950s and 1960s and to make a fresh start. It was the chance that was wasted to avoid the debt crisis.

But the countries which had such excellent export prospects became the most alluring clients for the banks, who pressed too many large loans upon them. Banks, as the old saw goes, prefer to lend to those who don't need the money. The vast majority of bank loans – 86 per cent of the total – went to oil-exporting countries and high-income 'developing' countries. Creditworthiness, by attracting too much new lending that was not really needed, contained the seeds of its own destruction. And the lending binge was cynically encouraged by the governments of the wealthy nations, because it suited their own economic needs in the wake of the oil shock.

17. The real effects of the oil shock

We have made the point that *neither* the Third World debt problem nor commercial bank lending to the Third World began with the oil shock of 1973–4. The shock was, however, a significant watershed for another reason. The major effect of the oil price rise was to reaffirm and make unmistakably clear the strong support of the US government, the other major industrial countries and the international financial institutions for the participation of commercial banks in this new form of capital transfer and debt build-up.

The new watchwords were 'recycling' and 'access'. The OECD, in its report on *Debt Problems of Developing Countries* in 1974, recommended 'freer access of developing countries to the capital markets of industrialised countries, e.g. by providing them some priority in queuing arrangements where these exist'.[183]

The International Monetary Fund, in its Annual Report for 1975, found that the

> investment of the surpluses of oil exporting countries in national and international financial markets – together with the expansion of international financing (through both bilateral arrangements and multilateral facilities) has resulted in a *satisfactory* channeling of funds into the current account deficits of the oil importing countries.[184]

With the same type of doublethink we saw in the World Bank annual surveys of debt in the 1960s, the IMF advocated both more concessional lending (to improve the debt service profile) and more private lending (which would boost immediate gross flows but worsen the debt service profile). It warned:

> For countries with the most severely strained borrowing capabilities, the need for larger flows of concessional aid is urgent, and maintenance of the net inflow of private capital at its high 1974 level will require both care on the part of the borrowing countries to follow policies that defend their creditworthiness and cooperative efforts by capital exporting countries to encourage the needed flows of financial assistance.[185]

In the entire annual report that year, the IMF did not say one word about the need for 'adjustment' to the new, higher oil prices, or for belt-tightening on the part of debtor countries. A Fund official later explained: 'The concern at that time was that countries should not attempt to adjust too quickly, on the grounds that such an attempt, if collectively pursued, could lead to an undesirable deepening of global recession.'[186]

US Secretary of State Henry Kissinger addressed the Seventh Special Session of the UN General Assembly on 1 September, 1975. He brought the same message. The most successful developing countries, he said, the ones that no longer require concessional aid, depend heavily on borrowing in the private capital markets.

> Their future access must be assured.
>
> We must now find new ways to enhance the opportunities of developing countries in the competition for capital. And we need to match in new ways potential sources of capital with the investment needs of developing countries.[187]

Kissinger suggested three ways of promoting this access to private capital markets: a quadrupling of capital for the World Bank's International Finance Corporation affiliate; the creation of a 'trust' which would attract new capital for investments in developing countries, supported by a $200 million loss reserve provided by governments; active assistance to the work of the IMF–World Bank Development Committee 'to find ways to assist developing countries in their direct borrowing in the capital markets'.

> Finally, we believe that all industrial countries should systematically review the conditions for developing-country access to their national markets. . . . The United States is prepared to provide technical assistance and expertise to developing countries ready to enter long-term capital markets, and we ask others to join us.[188]

With such a ringing endorsement, it is not surprising that bankers assumed they would be rescued if they got into trouble.

> Nothing like an 'official guarantee' could be deduced explicitly from the statements of Western public figures, but there is no doubt that the encouragement of the recycling of OPEC surpluses by the world's leading monetary authorities appeared to corroborate this assumption of the bankers. *Official concern focused only on the fearful consequences for world trade and political stability if the lending did not occur and the purchasing power of the Third World were to be suddenly diminished.*[189]

The reason for this official enthusiasm for lending to the Third World is reasonably clear as well. One effect of the oil price rise had been to put pressure on the balance of payments of the petroleum-dependent economies of the developed countries. Japan was particularly threatened, since it was poor in local energy resources and dependent on export earnings for its necessary imports, but the United States and the European countries were also forced to make adjustments in their balance of payments. 'With all the major industrial nations trying for current account surpluses (or at least to avoid deficits) and with OPEC countries recording their own surpluses, debts are left for others.'[190]

Two further points must be made. First, it was not just the commercial banks that expanded their lending after the oil shock. The International Monetary Fund and the World Bank also participated in the 'recycling' merry-go-round, borrowing billions of dollars from the oil exporting states with large payments surpluses and relending the money to Third World clients. The IMF set up a special 'Oil Facility' designed to help countries finance their oil import burdens.

Using the rhetoric of aiding the 'poorest of the poor', and providing 'basic needs', McNamara massively expanded the lending of the World Bank (which in 1970 had its own negative net transfer problem; that is, it had collected more in debt service on old loans than it had lent in new money). Countries that were so obviously uncreditworthy that even the banks wouldn't touch them (a small and shrinking category in the 1970s, as banks tried to diversify their risk by lending to as many different countries as possible) were able to get funds from the IMF and the World Bank.

The export credit agencies of the creditor countries also enthusiastically expanded their lending to the Third World. In doing this these countries were trying to maintain or restore balance in their own trade accounts by pushing off on the Third World the deficits they were unwilling to accept for their own countries.

The critical point is this: no one was telling Third World countries that they had to 'adjust' their spending and consumption to the new, and much higher, price of oil, even though the belief was nearly universal at that time that oil prices would stay high permanently. Net *importers* of oil were encouraged to borrow to cover their deficits, rather than cutting back on ambitious development plans. Net *exporters* of oil were encouraged to borrow because their projected export earnings looked great. There was something more going on than the price of oil.

18. Firefighters or arsonists?

The increase in prices of Third World exports and the enormous flows of credit in the early and mid-1970s temporarily halted the parade of debtors to the Paris Club for rescheduling, but some uneasiness about their creditworthiness remained. This malaise was suppressed by near-universal confidence on the part of creditors that the International Monetary Fund and the World Bank knew how to supervise their clients' borrowing. So long as either or both of these institutions could vouch for the credit of governments who were taking their advice, it was thought, creditors would be safe.

All debtors who came to the Paris Club for rescheduling were required to sign an IMF stand-by agreement,[191] which was also the condition for new aid. The IMF played a critical role in Paris Club renegotiations, officially certifying the existence of 'imminent default' and prescribing a foreign exchange budget that specified the amount each country would need to borrow. This gave the Fund enormous power over both the supplicant country and the creditors.

> Use of the IMF's projections avoids haggling over whether sources could be higher and uses lower, because the IMF's projections are deemed to reflect an objective assessment of the outlook in the context of the best politically feasible policy mix.[192]

By 1975, commercial bank loan contracts routinely included the requirement that the borrowing government remain in good standing with the IMF, and after some hard experience this was refined to provide that the termination of a stand-by or extended arrangement with the Fund would constitute an event of default.[193] This reliance on the IMF was only enhanced when one or more debtors ran into debt problems requiring a rescheduling, although the failure of IMF supervision to prevent the emergence of such problems should have given the creditors pause.

This reliance by all creditors on the IMF's 'seal of approval' of course gave that agency enormous power. The managing director of the Fund boasted as early as 1973 that:

> Fund financing has had an important effect in restoring confidence on the part of other lenders and thereby unlocking access by the country concerned

to additional external finance. It has been estimated that every dollar of Fund financing in support of adjustment programs has in the recent past generated an additional four dollars of new commercial lending.[194]

Few if any of the banks bothered to do their own check on creditworthiness as long as the IMF encouraged them to lend. In 1979 the Philippines became the first country to complete the full three-year term of an IMF Extended Fund Facility (EFF), a new type of program supposed to provide strict supervision over a longer period of adjustment than the traditional one-year stand-by program.

The program was a miserable failure, judged on its own terms. According to a confidential Fund evaluation of the program, the Philippines missed virtually all the economic targets that had been agreed between it and the Fund. The IMF's requirements, including both the floor on foreign reserve holdings and the ceilings on domestic and foreign loans, all had to be revised. Nevertheless, the IMF insisted that the program was a success. The *Asian Wall Street Journal* reported that

> banks will make government-guaranteed loans to the Philippines almost blindly as long as the IMF doesn't withdraw its support . . . any IMF judgment on Philippine economic health becomes tantamount to a self-fulfilling prophecy. The IMF can help the Philippines prosper simply by suggesting that it expects the nation to do so. Banks will then continue the essential loans.[195]

The Fund would never publicly acknowledge what one of its former officials, Irving Friedman, admitted to a reporter:

> [T]he Fund can't be giving danger signals, warning bells to all these private institutions. Because if you're worried about a country, what you're trying to do is help the country eliminate the problem. You're not trying to advertise the problem. Because if the Fund did advertise it, it would be responsible for a self-fulfilling prophecy.[196]

Some of the bankers suspected that the IMF did not know everything about maintaining a healthy balance of payments, but after one bruising experience when a syndicate headed by Citibank tried to discipline Peru without the mediation of the IMF, the banks decided that they preferred to let the Fund do the supervising. After all, they could not be faulted by their shareholders if they accepted the near-universal belief in the IMF as the highest repository of balance-of-payments wisdom.

We have already seen that the standard IMF formula for an austerity program contained some very strange methods for solving a debt crisis, i.e. liberalisation (rather than budgeting and conservation) of foreign exchange, and making up the difference through new borrowing which was usually larger than that which had led to the initial problem. In this way old crises were patched over, but not solved, in ways which led to new crises. But the IMF's role went beyond this. It also devoted a lot of energy to persuading countries which had *low* debt burdens and were *not* in any type of imminent default or crisis to liberalise controls and to begin massive borrowing. Following this advice led some of these countries into a crisis which was the logical effect of the IMF advice they had received.

The Fund and Bank, in fact, seemed to be following a deliberate strategy of luring countries that had low debt burdens into heavier borrowing. Some governments were suspicious of dealing with the Fund because they had observed the political, social and economic disruption that accompanied Fund-sponsored stabilisation programs in other countries. Others simply wished not to borrow heavily, especially on the relatively expensive terms of commercial bank loans. These wary governments were wooed by the Fund with what might be called 'special introductory offers' – loans with only light conditionality attached, where the most worrisome effect of the program was in fact a radical increase in the country's rate of indebtedness.

A few specific country case studies which the author has personally investigated will illustrate this very serious accusation.

Tanzania, a country which was noted for its attempt to build an indigenous African variety of socialism, received an IMF loan with light conditionality in 1974. The loan helped Tanzania over a temporary crisis and, as one cabinet member expressed it, 'we got used to living with the tiger.' By 1977 the crisis had passed and Tanzania had a comfortable 'cushion' of foreign exchange reserves equal to five months' worth of imports (three months' worth is usually considered more than adequate).

At this point the IMF, in routine consultations, advised Tanzanian leaders that their reserves were 'embarrassingly large' and might lead the country's aid donors to reduce their contributions. A poor country, the Fund (and the World Bank) argued, should not hoard its reserves but spend them in order to develop more rapidly. They persuaded the government to abolish the foreign exchange budgeting system, called 'confinement', and lift controls on imports.

A substantial proportion of the money thus 'deconfined' was spent on non-essential consumer goods. The result was a rapid and drastic depletion of foreign exchange, which led to a new foreign exchange crisis within half a year. By the end of 1978 Tanzania's reserves were sufficient to cover only *ten days'* worth of imports, compared to the three-months supply at the end of the previous year. This time Tanzania was forced to negotiate with the IMF and Bank – difficult, extended negotiations which eventuated in the early 1980s in the virtual dismantling of Tanzania's version of 'socialism'.

This bizarre episode left a legacy of bitterness among Tanzanian officials, many of whom were convinced that the Fund (and Bank) were virtually creating a crisis which gave them power over the Tanzanian government.[197]

Another self-styled 'socialist' government suspicious of IMF austerity programs was that of Michael Manley's Jamaica. In 1977, however, Manley rejected the advice of his party's left wing, who argued that to deal with the IMF would be a betrayal of the voters who had just reelected him. He then signed an 'easy' agreement with the IMF which opened the gates to more commercial bank borrowing. As in Tanzania, the country was in a new crisis within two years, and the loans which had been received in the interim meant that the debt was heavier and the government had fewer options for dealing with it. The conditions for a new IMF program in 1979–80 were so harsh that Manley lost legitimacy with the voters of Jamaica and could not win the election of 1980, despite a last-moment repudiation of the IMF by his party.[198]

India provides yet another example, and because of the wealth of documentation perhaps the clearest, of a country seduced into debt by the IMF. In 1981 the Fund agreed to lend India nearly $6 billion, the largest single IMF loan to that date, as part of a three-year Extended Fund Facility.

No crisis justified this huge borrowing. The World Bank remarked that at the time the loan was negotiated 'Reserves were at record levels and there was a significant pipeline of concessional assistance which had built up at the same time that the debt service burden had fallen to its lowest level in two decades.'[199] The IMF itself congratulated India for seeking assistance *before* the economy fell into dire straits. 'As one official put it, "the agency wants countries to come in before the situation is desperate." He added, "India is not a basket case. But do you want only basket cases to come in?"'[200]

Since India had a foreign debt of roughly $16 billion in 1981, almost entirely composed of official credit on concessional terms, it could be easily calculated that the IMF loan alone would increase that debt by one-third. But the IMF loan also opened the door to additional lending, functioning as a sort of bridging loan until much larger amounts of commercial, World Bank and other types of finance could be put into place. 'Substantial additional borrowing, much of it on commercial terms, will be required . . . until adjustment is complete,' the IMF asserted.[201]

The *quid pro quo* for the India agreement was not austerity, but import liberalisation and improvement of conditions for foreign investment. In fact, the only balance of payments problem which could be diagnosed for India at the time of the loan in 1981 was *a widening trade deficit which was largely due to liberalisation measures already taken at the instigation of the Fund.* Just as with Tanzania, the IMF had threatened that government donors might reduce aid to a country that hoarded its reserves, and this warning had been one impetus to the liberalisation which had begun in 1977. The IMF loan was a bribe to persuade India to carry on rather than to halt or reverse liberalisation because of fears of a foreign exchange shortage.

> The import policy of the past three years has provided a framework for assuring fuller utilization of capacity and removing the petty obstructions to imported inputs not produced in India. Maintaining this environment *in the face of severe deterioration of the trade account* provides ample evidence of the Government's commitment to a more open economic environment and provides a solid foundation for further improvements.[202]

India was not a 'basket case' when it contracted the IMF loan, but it may well be before the flood of borrowing contracted in the 1980s is paid off. The country's total debt burden was recently estimated at $70 billion. While the IMF memorandum approving the loan predicted that debt service payments would 'peak' at 16 per cent of current receipts in the late 1980s, the World Bank more recently forecast a ratio close to 20 per cent in 1990 and warned that unless exports grow faster, it could top 40 per cent in 1995. If only hard-currency receipts are counted, the debt service ratio is already in the mid-twenties.

With debt service rising and net new flows of aid negligible, the Fund and Bank are getting tougher in their insistence on completion of the program of liberalisation. The next IMF agreement India signs may not have such easy conditions as that earlier one.

As in the case of India, the IMF Extended Fund Facility (EFF) loan extended to Sri Lanka in 1977 was not a response to crisis, but to 'disappointing but positive economic performance, and irksome but not chronic balance of payments constraint'.[203] It was, as in India, an inducement to open up a closed economy to imports from Western creditors and to increased foreign investment.

The policy reversal, supported by large foreign loans from the World Bank's soft-loan facility, other official aid flows and commercial credits, liberalised imports and unleashed an inflow of imported consumer goods. It promoted foreign investment and spurred a construction boom of tourist hotels and office buildings.

Rising tension between the two major ethnic groups on the island, Singhalese and Tamils, broke out into open warfare in 1984. Some Sri Lankans attributed the communal violence to the economic changes introduced in 1977, which affected the economic fortunes of the two groups quite unevenly. The racial violence had a devastating impact on the government's hopes for a 'Singapore-style' economic development. Production was disrupted, foreign investors and private foreign lenders were scared away and defence spending crippled the government's ability to make economic investments.

The economic problems forced Sri Lanka to negotiate with the IMF in 1986. Export performance has been too poor to cover the burden of debt service and therefore investment, growth and imports have had to bear the brunt of adjustment of the balance of payments.

Overoptimistic projections of economic trends and false promises as to what countries can expect of the world market are part of the arsenal of persuasion to overborrow. These projections include price estimates for specific commodities[204] and growth projections for the economy as a whole and for the export earnings for the specific countries they are advising.

> Bank growth projections for both output and trade have – year after year after year – turned out to be far higher than what was subsequently achieved. Rather than correcting this annual over-optimism, the Bank seems to have realized that few take the time to go back and check whether

> projections matched reality. *To the contrary, the high projections have served admirably to justify Bank policy prescriptions that have continued to urge export-oriented development.*[205]

The common thread of all four case studies – Tanzania, Jamaica, India and Sri Lanka – is that in all cases the IMF and World Bank loans and advice to borrow commercially *preceded* and, it is argued, caused or contributed heavily to the subsequent debt crises or problems.

In 1978 the World Bank advised Thailand to accelerate growth and termed its external deficits 'manageable'. Three years later it admitted that the expansionary measures it had urged had left the economy uncomfortably exposed to external shocks, and recommended to Thailand the debt supervision program of the Philippines. (We will see below how successful this was.) In 1986, however, the World Bank was again advocating an expansion of Thai borrowing in excess of the government's own debt ceilings, pointing out that Thailand's credit rating was the best in the Third World after China and Malaysia.[206]

China, like Tanzania and India, has felt pressure from the World Bank and IMF to spend its foreign exchange reserves in order to preserve its eligibility for concessional loans from the IDA. As the author wrote a few years ago,

> The utter hypocrisy of the Fund's expressions of concern about 'unsustainable' capital flows is nowhere better illustrated than in its behavior towards China and India. These two countries, dissimilar in political systems, are similar in having relatively self-contained economies and small proportions of foreign trade to GNP. Both countries have followed conservative policies towards foreign borrowing and reserve management and thus represent a challenge to the IMF spendthrift model. As admitted in the *1983 World Development Report* of the World Bank, this has enabled them to avoid the worst consequences of the 1980s trade recession.
>
> However, instead of applauding this responsible and sober pattern of exchange management, the IMF and the World Bank are nagging both countries to spend more and borrow more.[207]

The confidence on the part of commercial banks that the IMF would enforce 'ceilings' on the assumption of foreign debt, and thus assure the ability of the country to service all debt contracted, was badly misplaced. This point can be illustrated by the example of three countries where such ceilings were once supposedly in place.

The Philippines, the first Asian country to fall into *de facto* debt default, was actually considered a model of prudent debt management up to the very date of its default. The reputation for prudence rested on two factors. One was surveillance by the IMF, which has had a virtually unbroken string of stand-by arrangements with the Philippines since 1962. The other was a regulatory framework providing for central monitoring and control of foreign borrowing which was adopted by the legislature at the height of an earlier debt crisis in 1970.[208]

This debt-management system was progressively subverted in the years following its original passage. When first passed, the legislation placed an absolute ceiling of $1 billion on total governmental borrowing, with an annual ceiling of $250 million. Less than three months after he declared martial law (and did away with the legislature) in September 1972, Ferdinand Marcos amended the legislation by Presidential Decree. As amended, the overall ceiling now excluded Central Bank borrowing, and the annual ceiling was dropped. Other restrictions on the government's power to borrow were deleted or made more 'flexible'. Yet the IMF continued to cheerlead commercial bank lending to the Marcos regime, and gave that government credit for monitoring huge foreign borrowing to keep within its 'ceilings' as late as 1981, when the Fund and Bank were even recommending this system as a model to Thailand and other countries. The crisis broke two years later.

Indonesia was also supposed to abide by annual borrowing 'ceilings' specified by the IMF after its rescheduling and debt reorganisation in 1969. Yet these ceilings proved ineffective to prevent a completely uncontrolled binge of borrowing by Pertamina, its parastatal oil company which was run like a private kingdom, and the Indonesian government was forced to assume responsibility for the Pertamina debts in 1975.

In India the 1981 IMF program also included 'ceilings' on commercial borrowing, but these supposed 'ceilings' were far in excess of previous levels of borrowing and thus seem to have functioned more as an incitement to borrow than as a restriction on government wishes.

In fact, the type of debt monitoring which the IMF and World Bank claim to be carrying out cannot be enforced. Why should any country obey IMF-imposed borrowing 'ceilings' if it can obtain financing that exceeds the ceiling? The only real purpose of the 'ceilings' appears to have been to keep credit flowing by reassuring creditors that the country could handle its debt; but if the country can get credit anyway there is no incentive to observe the 'ceiling'. The idea contradicts its own premises. The only circumstance in which 'ceilings' could be reliably enforced is when the international community agrees that borrowing in excess of the agreed limits shall be automatically forgiven, but the creditors have never even considered that.

The IMF and the World Bank, which were touted by the creditor governments and banks as the institutions holding a monopoly of wisdom on how to put a debtor's financial house in order, were in reality inciting its clients to heavier spending and more borrowing. This subverted the borrowers' ability to service their debts in the long run, but in the short run it served perfectly the desires of the creditor governments which control those institutions to maximise their access to markets in the target countries. The Fund and Bank must be considered among the major perpetrators of the debt crisis.

19. Early warning signs

By the late 1970s, the signs of impending crisis were clear, although stoutly denied by the major parties. Some countries had already failed to pay timely debt service to the banks, which could have allowed the creditors to declare a default. That never happened[209] because nearly everyone was aware at this point that it was the creditors who had most to suffer if it did. Any formal declaration of default would trigger disorderly panic and a refusal by all creditors to roll over the principal of their loans when it came due. New lending would be out of the question. The bubble would burst, and creditors would lose all hope of collecting principal or interest.

Trouble showed up first in Zaire, an African country rich in strategic minerals, totally dependent on raw materials exports, and headed by a dictator reputed to be one of the richest and most corrupt in the world, but compliant in allowing European corporations to share the profits of the country's mineral exports. The Zaire crisis, in 1976, led to the formation of the 'London club', the commercial banks' analog to the 'Paris club' for rescheduling of debts to official creditors.

The 'solution' found for the Zaire crisis was a guide to the (immediate) future of Third World debt. Fearing that rescheduling would set a precedent that would be demanded by other troubled debtors, the banks (organised by Citibank's Irving Friedman, a veteran of the IMF and World Bank) instead offered Zaire a new loan which was exactly equal to the debt service Zaire was supposed to pay them. The banks were formally making a new loan, which supposedly signalled their confidence in the debtor, but *de facto* they were rolling over capital and lending the country the money with which it could pay themselves the interest. It was an expedient that was to be used in subequent debt crises, and in those later crises as in Zaire, it did not 'solve' anything, except the banks' need to preserve the fiction that their loans were good.

Peru presented the second problem case to the banks in 1977. Peru was unwilling to accept IMF conditionality; the banks were at first unwilling to reschedule without it. The banks, again organised under the aegis of Citibank, then agreed to make a new loan to the country and secured in exchange promises that the government would carry out IMF-like austerity measures. Not surprisingly, the people of Peru did not like such measures any more when the banks were exacting conditions than they did when the IMF was demanding them, and Peru did not fulfil the conditions. Thanks to rescheduling by official creditors in the Paris club, and to a revival of export earnings, Peru made a temporary recovery in the late 1970s which gave the creditors a false sense of security. But thereafter the banks insisted on each troubled country signing an IMF stand-by as a condition of rescheduling or new lending.

Jamaica, Turkey and Poland were other sovereign debtors who got into trouble before the 'big' debt crisis broke in 1982. But even before the crisis was officially recognised, *most of the money lent in the years 1978–82 was only replacing debt service taken out of the borrowers' economy.* Table 19.1 gives the picture.

Table 19.1
Amortisation and Interest as % of Disbursements
(Latin America)

1976	*1977*	*1978*	*1979*	*1980*	*1981*	*1982*	*1983*
48	65	53	71	63	75	106	135
Interest only as % of gross disbursements							
21	26	21	31	33	45	62	79

Source: Calculated from Inter-American Development Bank, *External Debt and Economic Development in Latin America* (1984) p. 19.

Another indicator of the coming crisis was the rise in the percentage of short-term debt to troubled borrowers. In normal times, short-term debt finances trade and causes few problems. But in the late 1970s and early 1980s, banks and borrowers conspired to use short-term debt to roll over long-term debt. The lenders, aware of the approaching crisis, were no longer willing to make five-year loans, but they considered themselves safe with three- or six-month exposures. Some Latin American borrowers, for their part, knew how to entice greedy lenders with high interest spreads.

> Desperate for money, the Latin countries were taking ever-increasing loans in the form of 'trade credits' beyond the volume of their trade, interbank lines, and overnight borrowing in the London market and in Fed Funds [the US interbank market – CP]. This activity drew into the net any number of lesser banks that had never been involved in foreign lending to any great extent, but went for the lure of very short – apparently very safe – loans at better than market interest rates.
>
> The big banks were the great villains. 'Why did you keep selling them Fed Funds?' asked the inquiring reporter of the treasurer of one of the ten largest banks, referring to his dealings with Mexico and Brazil. 'Well,' he said, 'they were paying an extra eighth [of a percent].' A corporate officer of another bank said he almost had to physically restrain his treasury people from

selling funds to the Latins because the spread on such transactions qualified the department for the bank's incentive bonus program.[210]

The third signal of the impending collapse of the Ponzi scheme was capital flight. Figures on capital flight are difficult to obtain because the activity is clandestine by nature. Estimates and inferences must be made by indirect methods, and by the time they reach the public the damage has been done.

It was only after the debt crisis broke in 1982 that economists woke up to the huge amounts of money that were spirited out of Latin America, the Philippines and other debtor countries in the 1970s and early 1980s. *Business Week* published the first assessment of this huge problem that reached the public, in 1983. That study estimated that more than $120 billion was shipped out of the so-called developing countries from 1975 to 1983 'to make

Table 19.2
Estimated Net Capital Flight (Cumulative Flows During 1976–85)
US$ billion. Minus sign indicates outflow

	Capital Flight		
	1976–82	*1983–85*	*Total*
Argentina	–27	1	–26
Bolivia	–1	0	–1
Brazil	–3	–7	–10
Chile	0	1	1
Colombia	0	0	0
Ecuador	–1	–1	–2
Mexico	–36	–17	–53
Peru	1	–1	0
Uruguay	–1	0	–1
Venezuela	–25	–6	–30
Subtotal	–93	–30	–123
India	–6	–4	–10
Indonesia	–6	1	–5
Korea	–6	–6	–12
Malaysia	–8	–4	–12
Nigeria	–7	–3	–10
Philippines	–7	–2	–9
South Africa	–13	–4	–17
Thailand	1	–1	0
Subtotal	–52	–23	–75
Total, 18 countries	–145	–53	–198

Due to rounding, columns and rows may not add.

Source: Morgan Guaranty Trust Company, *World Financial Markets*, March 1986, Table 10, p. 13.

investments ranging from Miami condominiums to deposits in numbered Swiss bank accounts'. In the three years 1980–82 alone – the climax of the debt bubble – $71 billion was spirited out of eight of the world's largest debtors (Brazil, Mexico, Argentina, Venezuela, Indonesia, Egypt, Philippines and Nigeria) while their debt increased by $102 billion.[211] In other words, 70 per cent of new borrowing in those critical years was 'used' for capital flight. For many of these countries, interest payments and capital flight together amounted to more than 100 per cent of the total of new lending.

A more recent appraisal of the scope of the problem appeared in the financial newsletter published by Morgan Guaranty Trust, one of the money centre banks. That study estimated capital flight indirectly as 'the counterpart of recorded net direct investments *plus* increases in gross external debt, *less* recorded outflows through current account deficits, and *less* the building up of foreign assets by the banking system and the official monetary authorities', and reached figures for the major debtor countries shown in table 19.2.

Another table in the same source spelled out the implications of capital flight for the debt burden, by juxtaposing the actual debt burden of certain countries (at the end of 1985) with the amount of debt they would have had if capital flight had not consumed the borrowed money (see table 19.3).

Table 19.3
Impact of Capital Flight on Debt
US$ billion, unless otherwise noted

	Gross external debt, end-1985		*Gross debt as percentage of exports of goods and services*	
	Actual	*Without capital flight*	*Actual*	*Without capital flight*
Argentina	50	1	493	16
Brazil	106	92	358	322
Mexico	97	12	327	61
Venezuela	31	–12	190	–55
Malaysia	20	4	103	18
Nigeria	19	7	161	62
Philippines	27	15	327	195
South Africa	24	1	131	15

Source: Morgan Guaranty Trust Company, *World Financial Markets*, March 1986, Table 12, p. 15.

'On the admittedly oversimplified assumption that capital flight served only to inflate debt buildup and related interest charges, several of the [countries in table 19.3] might have been practically debt-free today – were it not for capital flight,' the newsletter commented. But it is even worse than these figures show. As James Boyce has pointed out,[212] none of the collected statistics on capital flight include interest earned on capital transferred in earlier years, whereas interest is automatically added to debt totals if it is not paid promptly. Thus the actual contribution of capital flight to debt is understated in these tables.

All of the published reports appeared after the crisis broke in 1982. The banks, however, knew about the capital flight before they read it in *Business Week*, because *they were soliciting and accepting it as deposits.* 'International private banking' is the euphemism for the wooing of large deposits from very wealthy Latin Americans, Africans and Asians. The same institutions which were, by 1982, reluctant to make new loans to the most heavily indebted governments in the Third World, showed no reluctance to accept private deposits from the members of those governments. Citibank, Morgan Guaranty, Bank of America and Chase are the most active in 'international private banking' to wealthy Mexicans. Citibank, according to James Henry, is the most aggressive American bank in that area, just as it was the most aggressive in 'sovereign risk' lending.[213]

In fact, Henry concludes, the United States as a whole is almost certainly a net debtor of all these countries, since it holds a larger percentage of their private deposits than it does of their international debt. 'Thus the basic role played by US banks to Latin America was that of a middleman between the short-term deposits of the countries' elites and the medium-term loans demanded by their governments.'[214]

But while many people were aware by the early 1980s that the debt juggernaut was out of control, the leading bankers and the international institutions were publicly declaring their confidence as loudly as they could. This was not because they did not know better. The metaphor of the Ponzi scheme suggests another explanation for the enthusiastic hype about Third World lending that continued throughout the 1970s.

If the big banks *knew* that their Third World loans were going sour, they had a strong incentive to conceal that fact and lure more players into the con game. Like Tom Sawyer contemplating the fence he had to whitewash, their interest lay in convincing their supposed rivals that it was a highly profitable business with negligible risk.

'During the 1970s, the number of institutions participating in loan syndications increased more than tenfold. This meant that many small and medium-sized banks, with little or no previous experience in sovereign lending, became active in the market.'[215] The smaller banks relied on the reputation and expertise of the big banks, who were the ones who organised and led the jumbo loans syndications, and on the information provided to them by these larger banks.

> The risk analysis done at the large money-center banks differed both in form and content from that provided to newly participating institutions, however. *The internal documents prepared at the money-center banks were much more elaborate, detailed, and candid than the information memoranda used to make the sales pitch associated with a loan syndication. . .*
>
> Clearly, the content and quality of the bank's information memoranda

> were more critical in the decision processes of regional banks than of the money centers. *Viewed objectively, the memoranda were written as sales documents* . . . and were primarily intended as a formality. *They served to pave the way for a decision that was in large part already taken: to increase international exposure.*[216]

There was even some suspicion that the big banks were quietly reducing their own exposure in some of the same countries whose 'creditworthiness' they were extolling to other, smaller banks. Citibank was suspected of such behaviour in Bolivia in 1978, for example.[217]

The reason was simple: the more new money that *other* banks could be induced to pour into these already overborrowed countries, the more free foreign exchange the debtor countries would have with which to service their old debts. Added to this was the prospect of easy profits to be made from risk-free syndication and management fees charged to the other institutions which were actually putting their money in jeopardy.

In June 1981, Walter Wriston, chairman of Citibank, suggested at a meeting of the American Bankers Association that Latin American lending was so risk-free that commercial banks could safely *treble* the proportion of their total assets represented by loans to developing countries, from 5 to 15 per cent.

Rescheduling, a Citibank publication suggested in 1980, actually enhanced the profitability of Third World lending:

> Since World War II, defaults by LDC's, when they have occurred, have not normally involved major losses to the lending banks. Defaults are typically followed by an arrangement between the government of the debtor country and its foreign creditors to reschedule the debt. . . . Since interest rates or spreads are typically increased when a loan is rescheduled, *the loan's present discounted value may well be higher than that of the original credit*.[218]

The cheerleading continued right to the brink of the crisis. The IMF and the World Bank published a report on private lending on 5 April 1982, just weeks before Mexico announced it could not service its debts. The conclusion of this report was that 'there is considerable scope for sustained additional borrowing to increase productive capacity'. If 'the market' got too worried about any particular client, the interest rate spreads could be raised to make it more profitable.[219]

In the winter of 1981–2, however, gross new lending by banks to Latin America began to decline. As debt service continued to rise – accelerated by a steep rise in interest rates as the US Fed tried to control inflation with tight money and by the drastically shortened maturities we have already mentioned – Latin America reached its 'break-even point' and began to ship out more money in debt service than it received in new lending (see Figure 2.1, p. 13). Not coincidentally, the defaults began at the same time. Mexico declared itself unable to make debt service payments in August 1982. Brazil declared bankruptcy in December 1982. Even earlier than these (but little noticed because at first it seemed an exceptional case) Argentina had halted debt service during the Falklands War. The Ponzi scheme had reached its limits. The bubble had burst. The debt crisis had officially arrived.

20. The IMF non-solution

At first the US authorities tried to handle the Mexican and Brazilian debt crises along the old lines. For three years, from 1982 to 1985, an attempt was made to use the tools which had worked in previous decades: rescheduling sanctioned by the creditors, conditionality enforced by the IMF, and new money as the reward for accepting conditionality. It was quickly recognised, however, that the dominant role of the commercial banks in Latin America and the huge sums involved required some new departures.

Before 1982, official creditors, who were spending taxpayers' money, were able to show flexibility not only in rescheduling debt but also in lending new money, which more than covered the debt service due. The sums which would have been necessary to bail out creditors in 1982, however, were far beyond the ability of official creditors to provide, given the political restraints within which they worked.

Moreover, US banks did not operate in the same fashion as the Paris Club. Unwise as their lending pattern had been in the 1970s, the banks had finally reached the limit beyond which they were unwilling to make new loans. There was also an important difference between the interests of the largest money-centre banks and those of the regional and smaller banks which had been brought into Third World lending through syndicated loans organised by the big banks. The very survival of the largest banks was threatened by the *de facto* default of Mexico and Brazil. The regional and smaller US banks, however, were not so exposed and could afford to take the loss. They began to realise that they had been 'taken', lured into the Ponzi scheme. They wanted to pull out of Third World lending, take their losses, and go back to their other, domestic, business.

But if the thousands of smaller banks that had been recruited by the big banks into syndicated loans were allowed to pull out of the game, the bubble would collapse with a bang, and the largest banks would collapse with it. In another of the many ironies of the debt crisis, the banks were tangled in one of the legal instruments devised as a measure to protect themselves from loss. If *any* bank, even a small one, were to declare a default and attempt to seize assets, the entire complex of cross-default clauses inserted into all loan agreements would be activated, triggering a free-for-all scramble for non-existent assets to offset against the loan. And if several banks, even small ones, declared their

Latin American loans in default, banking regulators could hardly recognise the same loans as sound ones on the big banks' asset sheets. The small banks had to be forced to stay in the game.

To deal with the crisis, an informal creditors' cartel was organised. The key elements in this creditors' cartel were the US Treasury, the US Federal Reserve Board, the largest commercial banks in the United States, Europe and Japan, and the International Monetary Fund. The purpose of the creditors' cartel was to exercise discipline in two directions: over the delinquent debtor governments, and over the thousands of smaller banks who had joined syndicated loans organised by the big banks or who had independently made loans to the same borrowers.

Most of the elements for dealing with the Mexican and Brazilian debt crisis (which became generalised for Latin America as banks stopped new lending to all countries in the continent) were holdovers from the reschedulings of the 1960s and 1970s. They included:

- Rescheduling of principal. The article of faith that countries never have to repay principal was reaffirmed. (Since debtors could not even meet interest payments, there was really no other option.)
- New lending to help debtors pay their interest payments.
- Acceptance of IMF conditionality by debtor nations as the price of rescheduling and new lending.

The presence of commercial banks among the creditors required some innovations that were peculiar to the post-1982 period, however. Commercial banks did not behave like official creditors. They were private businesses, and thus extremely loath to continue lending once the old loans had soured; they were also subject to fairly rigid regulatory rule by several US government agencies. Therefore, two new devices were made part of the crisis management canon:

- Interest payments from debtors to banks had to be kept up to date. If interest payments were delayed for more than ninety days, regulations required the banks to list the loans as 'nonaccruing'. This acknowledgement of probable losses would make it difficult to justify new lending, and new lending was an essential component of the strategy, because (to complete the circle) it enabled the debtors to keep interest payments up to date.
- Banks had to be forced by governments *not* to declare default and not to try to pull their money (principal) out. In addition, they had to be forced to lend new money to the country.

'Forced lending' was a genuine novelty. For the big banks, it was both the price of official support (partial bail-outs in the form of new lending from the international financial institutions) and a matter of self-preservation. For the smaller banks, it was a nuisance and an outrage, a violation of the sound principle that good money should not be thrown after bad. It could be enforced only with the aid of pressure from the US Fed, the Bank of England and other central banks, which threatened to come down harshly on the banks it regulated if they did not play ball.[220] Even with this muscle behind it, the enforcement was incomplete. There was a gradual attrition of smaller banks from the creditors' cartel.

The IMF's managing director, Jacques de Larosière, announced the policy of forced lending at a meeting of creditor banks shortly after the Mexican default. By requiring banks to lend as new money a certain percentage of their existing exposure to each country (initially seven per cent for Mexico and Brazil), the authorities could deflect criticism that they were 'bailing out the banks', and claim instead, as de Larosière did, that they were 'bailing in' the banks.

The official line legitimising this unorthodox behaviour was that the money was not really lost; the debt crisis was only temporary, a 'liquidity' problem rather than a 'solvency' problem. This theory was pushed hard by the IMF, the World Bank, the Federal Reserve Board, the US Treasury and the large commercial banks – all members of the creditors' cartel. The supposedly independent Institute for International Economics supported this official line with projections of future economic growth and future new lending which assumed away the problem: they assumed, for example, that the developed industrial countries would enjoy steady growth and that massive new flows of capital would be attracted to the ailing debtor countries.[221]

There were many problems with this strategy. The most important was that new money was not flowing spontaneously to the troubled debtors – the best indication that the banks themselves did not believe the line they were pushing about the crisis being only temporary. The sums raised through the technique of 'forced lending' were not only insufficient to cover the total debt service due from the debtors; they were not even sufficient to cover the interest payments which, according to the strategy, had to be paid promptly. The debtor countries were thus outraged that the 'unwritten agreement' that they should always receive net inflows of capital had been broken, while bank analysts shook their heads in dismay as banks continued to *increase* their exposure to those problem debtors.

Just as Citibank had predicted in 1980 (see *supra*, p. 88), the banks took advantage of the strategy to raise interest rates and 'front-end fees' at every rescheduling. Just as they had first been attracted into Third World lending by the high spreads they could charge justified by the 'risk' of lending, so they now jacked up their profits in the short run by increasing their exposure to their most dubious debtors.

The hubris of the bankers was noted with some anger by members of the US Congress. In 1983 the Congress debated an increase in the quota of the IMF. The increased quota was mandatory if the Fund were to continue to play its role as policeman of the debt crisis; indeed the increase turned out to be, as some predicted, far too small for the role assigned to the Fund.

A strange alliance of free-market conservatives and left liberals nearly defeated the quota increase, and it squeaked through in the end only because the Reagan administration solemnly warned that the alternative was worldwide financial catastrophe. But one price exacted by Congress in exchange for approving the quota increase was a law forbidding the banks to take their rescheduling fees into profits immediately. This rule made the fees much less attractive as a boost to current profits, and the practice of charging them ceased.

The Latin debtors grumbled, gathered together periodically in one forum or another to call for debt relief, and did not always pay their interest when it was due. Nor did the debtor countries abide by the conditions they accepted in order to receive IMF standby credits and the larger loans from other sources which were unlocked by the IMF seal of approval. Brazil signed no less than five agreements with the IMF in 1983, none of which were fulfilled. Indeed, one of the most ironic aspects of the debt crisis was the process by which the authority of the IMF, which in appearance was elevated practically to the role of a global dictator, was in fact subverted and eroded by its very centrality.

This happened because the IMF was made the gatekeeper of a system which worked more for the benefit of the creditors than the debtors. By the rules of the game which they had themselves decreed, the creditors should cut off new money to a country that failed to follow its IMF austerity program. But if they did cut off the new money, the debtor would be unable (and certainly unwilling) to pay them the interest which maintained the fiction that the loans were still 'performing'. This in turn would trigger the default and collapse which the creditors feared. The creditors were more hostage to the IMF than were the debtors. This led inevitably to an erosion of conditionality.

This was underlined in the summer of 1985 when Argentina devised its own austerity program, combined with a currency reform creating a new unit of money, the austral. The program included wage and price controls, which are usually not permitted by the IMF. The Argentines presented the IMF with a *fait accompli* and asked the IMF to endorse their own reform. In theory, this is what the IMF always does; it is a convenient fiction that austerity plans are always designed by member governments and represent their own policy choices rather than IMF dictation. When the Argentines actually did devise their own plan, they had to appeal over the heads of the IMF to key US government officials, who sent word to the IMF that it should approve the Argentine plan.

On another front the IMF and the World Bank were losing credibility. In the poor countries dependent more on official than on commercial bank finance, the IMF and the World Bank were major lenders. Ever since the Bretton Woods institutions were formed, they have insisted on the status of preferred creditors. If a nation failed to service its debts to the Bank and Fund on time, so the theory went, it would never get a penny from other creditors. But in the autumn of 1984 rumours began to circulate that literally dozens of nations, mostly in Africa, were failing to repay the IMF on time. As we might expect from our Ponzi scheme metaphor, their net transfer *with the IMF* had become negative. They could not expect to receive new money in the same amounts as repayments were due. Only a year after the hard-won quota increase, the IMF itself was running out of money.

21. The Baker plan and Structural Adjustment

With the IMF strategy failing, in September 1985 US Treasury Secretary James Baker announced a shift in the officially sanctioned debt strategy of the creditors' cartel.

The Baker plan handled the crisis of legitimacy of the IMF by turning the spotlight on the World Bank. As the Fund had been the chief instrument for imposing policy changes on the Third World, it had acquired a well-deserved reputation for painful and counter-productive, even self-defeating austerity programs.[222] While the Fund was psychologically linked with austerity, the World Bank was associated with growth and capital inflows, and the Baker plan tried to cash in on this psychology. The Reagan administration was trying to co-opt the popular impatience with belt-tightening in the debtor countries. 'Take this down carefully,' George Shultz, US Secretary of State, told a Brazilian journalist who approached him after a speech in the UN: 'We support economic growth.'[223]

The plan in no way discarded the IMF gatekeeper role or IMF conditionality, however; instead it added another layer of conditionality which the World Bank had already been peddling for several years under the name of Structural Adjustment. The World Bank throughout its existence had dispensed capital liberally (too liberally in the opinion of some critics of both right and left) and had operated in an environment where other creditors were also throwing money at its member countries. In the wake of the debt crisis, however, it found the environment drastically changed.

The bulk of its loans were still extended for specific projects.[224] The money earmarked in this fashion could not be used to pay debt service, which was the crying need of governments (and their creditors) caught in the crisis. But worse, even the projects were now imperilled by lack of funds. Traditionally, the World Bank had required borrowing governments to commit their own resources in specified proportions to the projects it financed. But after the debt crisis broke, governments found that they could not allocate the needed domestic currency to World Bank-financed projects, because to do so they would be exceeding IMF-dictated ceilings on government expenditures!

A. W. Clausen came to the World Bank from the presidency of the commercial bank most vulnerable to Third World default (Bank of America), and at the end of his term (1981–6) he returned to it. Under his presidency, the

World Bank tried to cope with the new conditions by accelerating disbursements of foreign exchange and by financing a larger proportion of 'local costs' with foreign exchange which, traded for local currency, would then be available for debt service.

The importance of the Baker plan, however, was in the implication that existing limits on the amount of money lent under the Bank's Structural Adjustment program would be lifted. Structural Adjustment was the bank's analog to IMF balance-of-payments credits. Indeed, after the IMF introduced its three-year loan program called the Extended Fund Facility, it had become difficult to distinguish analytically between the Bank's Structural Adjustment lending and the IMF's EFF.

Structural Adjustment Loans (SALs) had first been introduced by the World Bank in 1980, before the debt crisis broke, as

> . . . one response in an effort to help supplement, with longer-term finance, the relatively short-term finance available from the commercial banks and the resources available from the IMF in order that the current account deficits of many developing countries do not become so large as to jeopardize seriously the implementation of current investment programs and foreign-exchange producing activities.[225]

They represented an evolution of the Bank's sector and program loans and an ambitious effort to expand and deepen the already impressive control exercised by the international financial institutions over policy choices in borrowing countries.

> Previous program lending, however, has generally been designed to meet the immediate consequences of crises. . . . As a result, the programs supported were concentrated on measures dealing with immediate difficulties rather than on finding solutions to a country's underlying, long-term structural problems. Structural adjustment lending, on the other hand, envisages the probability of multiyear programs being worked out and supported by a succession of loans. Because such lending will be developed with long-term objectives in mind, it is expected to have more enduring effects than the crisis-oriented operations that were characteristic of the Bank's program lending in the past.[226]

The luxury of multi-year programs not geared to immediate crisis was not to be, however. The Bank, like the Fund, had failed to anticipate the debt crisis, or chose to conceal its forebodings with a false optimism in order to keep the Ponzi scheme going (see Chapter 19). (The Bank also predicted, incorrectly, that the price of oil would continue to rise in real terms in the 1980s.) A chapter on 'Bank Policies' in its 1982 *Annual Report*, issued just before the Mexican crisis, forcefully emphasised that commercially attractive borrowers should 'graduate' from concessional and Bank lending to higher-cost market-rate credits.[227] When the crisis broke, however, 'Structural Adjustment' policies were prescribed, without missing a beat, as the cure for the crisis.

The conditions attached to Bank program loans were perfectly complementary with IMF austerity programs, but they cut deeper and it was clearly intended that they should be more difficult to reverse than spending cuts. Whereas IMF programs are characterised as demand-oriented, focusing on measures such as cutting budget deficits and contracting the money supply which can be easily reversed once the crisis has passed, Structural Adjustment aspired to be a 'supply-side' conditionality aimed at nothing less than changing the economy's entire pattern of investment and production in ways that cannot be easily reversed. (In practice, however, the Bank and Fund conditionality may be virtually interchangeable.)[228]

'These loans do go to the heart of the political management of an economy,' a Bank vice-president admitted when the program was first announced. 'We will have to approach them with humility.'[229] But anyone who has had anything to do with the World Bank knows that humility is not their style. 'Negotiations' with debt-prostrated governments over the conditionality of Structural Adjustment have been carried out with the Bank's usual smug assumption of omniscience and perfect foresight.

The conditionality of Structural Adjustment Lending leaves no important sector of the borrower's economic life untouched: trade and exchange-rate policies, investment and operating policies for energy, agriculture and industry; the review of national investment priorities; the financial performance and efficiency of public-sector enterprises, the budget, tax policy, interest rates, and debt management.[230]

Underlying this plethora of specific conditions are the easily discernible forms of a few major objectives: 1. opening a closed or protected economy to world market forces through import and exchange liberalisation; 2. realigning prices within the economy to correspond to world market prices: 'getting prices right'; 3. privatisation of government economic enterprises; 4. reduction of labour's share in the national income.

Structural Adjustment conditionality, like the IMF conditionality discussed in Chapter 12, can be criticised as causing exactly the disastrous consequences which it is supposed to prevent. Import liberalisation is not the way to reduce imports, nor does it necessarily lead to increased production of exports.[231] Changing prices to benefit the 'agricultural sector' does not lead to more production (although the statistics may improve because sales are diverted from unofficial to official markets) but is likely to mean that poor people are less able to afford food to eat.[232] Industrial restructuring means the destruction of domestic industries for the benefit of foreign-owned conglomerates.[233] Privatisation means recolonisation (and permits the reduction of wages).[234] 'Institution building' means creating organs of authority that can bypass existing decision makers who resist the logic of externally imposed restructuring.[235] And one does not solve a debt crisis by forcing the borrower to assume yet more debt.[236]

On the contrary. As was argued earlier about IMF conditionality, World Bank style Structural Adjustment has in the real world *preceded* and, it can be argued, *caused* or contributed to a debt crisis more often and more reliably than it has ever cured one. If the major elements sound familiar – privatisation, market forces, repression of labour – they are. They were hallmarks of the Reagan revolution in the US economy, which resulted in large trade deficits and a huge US foreign debt which is still accumulating.

In the 'southern cone' countries of Latin America, Structural Adjustment was implemented even before the World Bank formalised the term in its lending program. Argentina, Uruguay and Chile adopted its main elements,

> (1) a policy of privatization of economic activities accompanied by a withdrawal of the state from its regulatory and developmental functions, (2) an opening up of the economy to international trade and financial flows, and (3) free market policies as regards price determination and capital markets . . . ,[237]

in the mid-1970s after rightwing military coups had swept away the legitimate governments of each nation. Although these countries enjoyed a short-lived prosperity fuelled by foreign borrowing in the latter part of the 1970s, they suffered debt crises like the rest of Latin America in 1982 – *after*, and in no small measure as a result of their implementation of Bank-prescribed Structural Adjustment.

The so-called Baker Plan had two separate prongs. For the fifteen 'most heavily indebted' nations (which included most of South America plus Mexico, the Philippines, Morocco, Nigeria and Yugoslavia) Baker proposed that the World Bank add $9 billion to its new lending over what had been projected for the following three years. Commercial banks were exhorted to boost their lending by $20 billion.

For the African and other low-income countries whose debt was owed primarily to governments and multinational institutions, Baker proposed a joint World Bank–IMF lending pool totalling $5 billion. The proposal suggested that $2.7 billion worth of repayments due to the IMF's Trust Fund should be channelled to countries in difficulty, and that the Fund and Bank should cooperate in enforcing conditionality on those countries.

One remarkable aspect of the Baker plan was the small amount of government finance which was offered. Aside from money funnelled from governments through the IMF and World Bank, the United States did not put up any of its own money. Rather, the commercial banks were again being asked to bail themselves out (or in) with new lending of $20 billion. A vague promise that the administration would look with favour on a future capital increase for the World Bank was the closest Baker came to pledging any new money.

The Baker plan was a cosmetic rather than a real change in strategy, a last-ditch attempt to maintain the fiction that the debt crisis was only temporary and could be surmounted if all parties cooperated under the direction of the creditors' cartel. All the major points of the first stage of debt crisis management (above) remained intact under the Baker plan. It proposed that everyone continue doing what they were supposed to have been doing anyway: the countries were to obey conditions laid down by the Fund and Bank, the commercial banks were to lend even more money to countries they well knew to be bad risks, and the US government would have its bank regulators help round up the restive small banks and wink at the carrying of Third World loans at full face value on bank balance sheets.

Sceptics noted that the sums offered to debtors under the Baker plan were probably insufficient to induce the desired behaviour. In comparison with the $29 billion extra which the commercial banks and the World Bank were supposed to lend in the following three years, the fifteen countries designated as beneficiaries of the Baker plan faced an interest bill of four times as much over the same period. The proposed IMF–World Bank joint fund for Africa was similarly sadly underfunded in relation to its mission of bailing out some $7 billion in arrears. When finally established, the Structural Adjustment Facility had only $3 billion to lend.

Even as the US administration continued to pretend that the Baker plan was 'working', Peru's president Alan García continued the unilateral limitation of interest payments he had inaugurated two months before the Baker plan was announced while other countries (Bolivia, Ecuador) fell more deeply into arrears. The largest debtor countries (Mexico, Argentina) used the threat of stopping interest payments as a means to extort more favourable conditions from their creditors. The Baker strategy, at base not very different from the one it replaced, was also failing.

22. Writeoffs

The debtor countries had called for debt relief ever since the crisis first broke. Finance Ministers made polite but impotent representations in private conferences. Fidel Castro stridently called for concerted repudiations. Presidential candidates in Argentina and Brazil ritually declared that the debt would not be paid through the hunger of their people (although the winning candidates went ahead and paid it anyway).

US Senator Bill Bradley was a different case. When he proposed that debt be written down by three per cent a year and – even more jolting to the banks – that interest rates also be reduced by three per cent, he was responding not to the pain of hungry people in Latin America but to American businesses and workers who had lost their markets in Latin America to the debt crisis. When the net transfer to Latin America changed from positive to negative, the orders which had kept American factories running during the 1970s diminished or disappeared. As the economists of the 1940s had foreseen, the transfer problem was fundamentally an *American* problem and it had finally come home to roost. The expanding financial universe had finally burst the skin of the bubble. The net transfer of capital from *south* to *north* (the payment of interest to the banks) could only be embodied in an import surplus for the United States, and it was hurting US business, and even more US labour.

Every dollar which had to be paid to the banks in debt service was a dollar not available to pay for imports from the US or elsewhere. Whereas lenders and exporters had enjoyed a symbiotic boom while the loans were flowing in the 1970s, the end of the boom put them in opposition to each other. In a clever op-ed piece for the *Wall Street Journal*, Henry Breck compared a conference at New York's Plaza Hotel in December 1986 to the climactic scene in the classic movie *The Maltese Falcon*, where Humphrey Bogart as Sam Spade engineers a split in the ranks of the criminals by insisting that they produce a 'fall guy'. In Breck's parody, Bradley was Bogey and the banks were doomed to be the fall guy. As in the original story, the choice of the fall guy was all the more satisfying because the scapegoat really had pulled the trigger and was, in addition, the least attractive member of the gang.[238]

The next phase of the debt crisis was initiated not by the US government but by Citibank. In the spring quarter of 1987, Citibank startled the financial world by announcing a $3 billion addition to its loan loss reserves, specifically against its exposure to troubled Third World debtors. With this step, the creditors' cartel lay shattered, the US was left without any debt policy (let alone a credible one) and the pretence that debt problems were just temporary was discarded. Most other banks quickly followed suit. They were no doubt speechless with fury at Citibank's coup, since Citibank had been the ringleader in the attempts to keep all other banks from taking any similar steps in the previous phase of the crisis.

Ostensibly Citibank's move was a reaction to Brazil's suspension of interest payments some weeks earlier. That was probably just the last straw, however. The supposedly successful conclusion of a rescheduling agreement with Mexico the previous autumn (weakly hailed as a success of the Baker plan!) had contained more seeds of destruction. Again, a debtor had forced the IMF and the banks to accept its own variation of an austerity plan. In the Mexico case the innovation was clauses which would trigger increased lending in case growth failed to reach a certain target or the price of oil fell below a specified level.

Other debtors immediately demanded from the banks terms as fine as those granted to Mexico. The banks insisted that Mexico was a special case but gave in later to Argentina, which angered the Philippine government into demanding a renegotiation of their just-signed agreement. Meanwhile, the task of persuading all the smaller banks that remained in the cartel to put up new money once again was scarcely possible.

Although the banks pretended that this move would allow them to take a tougher line against Third World debtors, the long-run effect was to confirm that the debt is unpayable. It was a small and still very inadequate start down the road to debt write-offs and eventual forgiveness, probably on the model of the settlement of pre-1917 Imperial Russian debts, pre-1911 and pre-1949 Chinese debts and the Latin American debts of the 1930s.

After the inauguration of George Bush as US president in 1989, the debtor countries and the financial world awaited the announcement of a new debt strategy with anticipation. The start of a new administration offered a sterling opportunity for a break with the ineffectual policies of the past, which had benefited only the short-term interests of the banks.

The 'Brady Plan', announced a few months later by Bush's Treasury Secretary, sounded good at first. While reaffirming most of the ingredients of US debt policy since 1982, the plan had two novel features. For the first time, the Administration publicly proclaimed the objective of *reducing* the debt load rather than increasing it, and encouraged banks to make debt reduction part of their rescheduling strategy.

Mexico, always the guinea pig for new debt strategies, was the test case for the Brady plan. And the eventual results of the Mexican rescheduling indicated that although the Bush administration might be facing in the right direction for a solution to the debt problem, for the present they were marching rapidly *backwards*.

The reason was simple: for the Brady strategy to work, the large banks had to be willing to swallow some losses on their Third World loans. But the government was undercutting this part of its strategy by the second novel feature of the plan: for the first time, public money would be available for a direct bail-out of the banks. It was a concession which the Reagan administration had adamantly refused to countenance, for all its sympathy for the big banks. And, for all the loud voices heard inveighing against a 'bank bail-out' just six years earlier (when resources for the IMF were increased) there was scarcely any public notice of this new policy.

The story can be told best by the *Wall Street Journal*:

> It may come as a shock, but the shaky foreign bank credits of Venezuela, the Philippines and Mexico have offered investors some of the best capital gains available the past few months.
>
> Those who bought Venezuelan bank loans at around 27 cents for each dollar of debt in early March now see prices hovering around 40 cents on the dollar, offering them a prospective 48% capital gain in little more than four months.
>
> The rebound has been fueled by the new U.S. debt strategy. Since the strategy was announced March 10, it has become increasingly clear that as much as $30 billion of public money will be made available to help the less-developed countries buy back their bank debts and enhance the value of the remaining ones. That has added to the value of the loans; for instance, the price for Polish bank debt has appreciated more than 20% since March 1.[239]

With such prospects of a bail-out, the banks had little incentive to accept losses on their loan portfolios and no appetite for the debt reduction part of the Brady Plan. Quite simply, the banks and Mexico could not agree on a price for discounting the old loans, and the large banks, which still had the alternative of 'new' lending to Mexico, happily resumed their old ways.

> The US-backed international debt strategy won't succeed unless big banks continue to lend to heavily indebted countries, bankers and debtor-country officials said.
>
> This is because the debt strategy has been modified to focus somewhat less on reducing the amount of debt outstanding and relatively more on seeking new bank loans for debtor countries. It also emphasizes cutting interest payments more than reducing debt principal.[240]

In the autumn of 1989, some banks took the reserve strategy to what many believed to be its inevitable conclusion: Morgan Guaranty Trust allocated reserves against 100 per cent of its Third World debt exposure, and other banks followed to the extent they could afford to do so. Nothing was as yet forgiven, but it was becoming clear which way the wind was blowing.

Part Three: Solutions

The title of this section must be taken as ironic. There are no simple solutions to difficult and complicated problems. And for many problems there are no solutions. Spilt milk cannot be drunk. Humpty Dumpty cannot be put back together again. The young man who is murdered cannot be brought back to life. His murderer cannot regain the years of life spent in prison. The best we can do in such cases is to clean up the spilt milk and broken eggs, punish the guilty (if we can agree on who they are), comfort the surviving victims and take measures to prevent the tragedy from happening again.

The first chapter in the conclusion to this book contains a discussion of the necessity of default, and a refutation of arguments against it. This is followed by a critique of the alternative 'solution' held out by the creditors' cartel as an example for Third World debtors to follow: the Asian export successes. Next, and most controversially, an attack is made on the prevailing idea that foreign capital contributes some almost magical quality leading to 'development', and it is argued that on the contrary, the conditions under which foreign capital can contribute to development are so strict that most real-life models cannot meet them. Finally, a few thoughts are offered on possible means to prevent a new debt problem arising in the future.

23. The case for repudiation

> Debt is not sacred. The USSR defaulted, China defaulted, American states defaulted, the Penn Central and the WPPSS defaulted. Default is as capitalist as apple pie.[241]

If the need for inflows of money from abroad has been greatly exaggerated (under the pretext that it is 'capital') the need for foreign exchange for trade is real enough, though much more modest than its propagandists would have us believe. All countries do need to trade, need to import goods which they do not make themselves, and for this they need a steady supply of foreign exchange – until they reach the stage when their own economy is so strong that its domestic currency is accepted everywhere. Even the United States needs foreign exchange with which to defend the exchange rate of the dollar.

This is the great irony and the great tragedy of the debt crisis. *In the name of the 'need for foreign capital' most of the countries of the Third World have been conned into loan contracts which are now draining foreign exchange out of their countries.* In the words of Argentinian economist Aldo Ferrer, countries which borrowed in previous decades in order to live 'beyond their means' are now being forced by the requirements of debt service to live 'below their means', that is, they are not even able to utilise all the funds which they can *earn* through their exports, tourism, etc. for the needs of their own economy.

If there is one thing upon which the vast majority of proposed 'solutions' to the debt crisis agree, it is the 'necessity' of getting capital flowing back to the Third World again. The banks use this as the clinching argument for why they should receive full payment on their loan contracts. 'If they don't pay us back, they'll never receive another penny of credit again,' they bluster. Another myth!

The truth is, as some more acute critics have pointed out, that they are not getting any net credit anyway; just the contrary. What is more, they will never get another penny of voluntary credit as long as they are bound to repay old creditors, and they will get very little new investment if the new investors fear that old creditors are going to claim all earnings which come to the country for many years to come. The name for this problem is the 'debt overhang'.

> Because foreigners correctly perceive this claim on future income, they

> will not lend even for new projects that would yield acceptable returns. This inability to insulate new claims from existing debt leaves countries in a vicious circle: they cannot restore creditworthiness without growth, and they cannot grow until creditworthiness is restored.[242]

The truth is that debtors will not receive any new voluntary credit *until the old credit is either repaid or otherwise extinguished.* Since there is no prospect (short of a catastrophic world hyperinflation) that it will be repaid within the next half century, it must somehow be extinguished.

This could be achieved by any of several methods. Debt–equity swaps, in which a quantity of debt, sold at a discount by a bank trying to cut its losses and clean up its asset portfolio, is exchanged for ownership of corporate assets in the debtor country, is the method currently favoured by the creditor cartel. Since host country resentment of foreign ownership and the capital drain caused by profit remittances (from Latin America in the 1960s) was one important reason for the massive shift into bank lending at the beginning of the 1970s, it is to be doubted that this represents a real solution, and its quantitative impact has thus far been marginal.

A far more promising field is the buy-back by debtor nations of their own discounted debt securities on the same secondary market. This allows the country to gain the full benefit of the reduced value of the debt, and it is the way much of the defaulted Latin American debt of the 1930s was eventually written down. In a little noted but highly significant development, Bolivia, the worst 'basket case' of Latin debtors, has been permitted by the creditors' cartel to buy back its own debt at market prices (because of Bolivia's inability to pay interest, priced at only eight to ten cents on the dollar).[243]

This is an extremely dangerous strategy for the creditors because of the perverse incentive built into it: the market price of debt depends not just on economic conditions in the debtor country but on the willingness to pay of its government, so in theory a declaration of default by one country could depress the price of its debt and allow a buy-back at bargain prices. It is clear that for the moment Bolivia is the only debtor encouraged to follow this strategy (it is not only *permitted* to do so but creditor governments are actually contributing aid to a fund created for this purpose) because its current government is subservient to creditors and otherwise following the wishes of the United States and the IMF.

It is possible, however, that the Bolivian model points the way to an eventual creditor-sponsored 'solution' of the debt crisis. This is the way much defaulted Latin American debt of the 1930s was eventually cleaned up.[244] If the Bolivian solution (or any variant which permits a lowering of the debt service-to-exports and debt sevice-to-GNP ratio) were to be selectively extended to other governments who demonstrated their willingness to comply with US and IMF-style requirements as to import and exchange liberalisation, foreign investment incentives, etc., the way would at least be cleared for modest amounts of new investment and a less modest restoration of exports from the United States and other creditor countries. Creditor governments might find this the most effective way to defuse the political time bomb of populist resentment and to strengthen their interests by rewarding and strengthening the conservative leadership which could most effectively guard the existing and potential interests of the creditors in the respective countries.

Lest anyone think that this is an optimistic assessment of the eventual outcome of the debt crisis, i.e. the reduction of debt service burdens to a level which would permit the resumption of investment and trade, it should be added that such measures will be taken not to help the peoples of the Third World but to avert the political threat which they now pose in all the major debtor countries (as epitomised by the strong showing of Cardenas in the recent Mexican elections and the near victory by 'Lula' in Brazil's).

The two best-known advocates of 'conciliatory default' have admitted as much:

> Perhaps the greatest danger which the debt crisis holds for the long-term interests of the United States and other industrialized countries is that the very adjustment that is strengthening the economies of many debtor countries will weaken their political and ideological bonds with the West.[245]
>
> We are heading in the direction I am advocating. The problem is, will we get there soon enough to get *political* credit for our actions?[246]

Debt forgiveness, in other words, has become *for the creditors* a compelling political necessity to stave off populist revolts which threaten to push ahead with more radical restructurings; and it will be selectively distributed as a reward to governments which accept the type of structural adjustment 'reforms' now being pushed by the World Bank and the Brady Plan. It will be used to purchase crude political advantage, as the US government used the debt problems of Costa Rica to coerce that would-be neutral country into *de facto* support of the Contra war against Nicaragua.[247] It will prove no panacea either for the dependence of Third World governments or for the poverty of their people, but exactly the contrary.

The Bradley Plan, which calls for the reduction of principal of old debts as well as the reduction of current interest payments on that principal, recognises this truth. The supporters of the Bradley Plan, chiefly exporters who wish to regain their lost markets in Latin America, want to get rid of the claims of old creditors which are blocking their access to these markets.

> 'The industrial countries have a real need to open up the less-developed countries,' says Lowell Bryan, a senior consultant on financial institutions at McKinsey & Co.. 'They need them as markets.'[248]
>
> [W]e need export markets. The logical markets are Central and South America; however, burdened with debt, they are really not able to purchase new equipment. If we resolve the debt problem . . . we will be able to create markets for U.S. exports and assist those nations to get their economies moving again.[249]

If the Plan is implemented, these businesses stand to gain a double advantage: not only will the reduction of old claims enhance the likelihood that they can do new business, but if the Plan is implemented as Bradley proposes, such forgiveness will be granted only to those countries that are willing to open their markets to foreign businesses. In this respect debt forgiveness would be subject to the same kind of conditionality that is now associated with IMF and World Bank loans.

There are two major problems with the Bradley Plan. The first is that this kind of 'solution' bears within itself the seeds of the *next* debt crisis. If the way is cleared for a new wave of lending, and simultaneously the debtor country is denied the right to control its own import bill, we are once more on the road to default. The cycle may take a half-century to complete (which seems to be the pattern since the early nineteenth century), but it may well go much faster if exchange controls and import substitution are not allowed; more likely, since the drain of exchange will be unremitting, development will never really get off the ground.

Another problem is that, despite its obvious common-sense appeal, the Bradley Plan itself has not been able to get off the ground, years after it was first proposed. If, as this book has argued from the outset, the negative flow of capital from the Third World represents a crisis for the creditor countries as well as the debtors, why have politicians in the United States been so slow to recognise the urgency of debt reduction?

We argued previously that the crisis had both a political and an economic dimension. The economic interest, however, is no longer as unambiguous as it used to be. In the immediate postwar decades it was in the economic interests of both US-based exporters and US labour to run an export surplus with the Third World. But the internationalisation of capital – the movement of manufacturing operations from the high-labour cost US mainland to export platforms in Latin America, the Caribbean and Asia – means that the interests of corporate owners are no longer bound up with the export surplus of the United States or other creditor countries.

The interests of capital and labour in this respect have been sundered, and the huge import surplus which the US ran in the 1980s was useful to capital in forcing give-backs and deunionisation on US labour. The political clout of labour in domestic politics has been correspondingly weakened, while the power of capital, and especially the banks, has been at its zenith in the 1980s but no longer depends economically on production based in the domestic economy.

The political imperative for extinguishing the debts persists, however. It could be done from one of two directions. If the market-oriented solutions discussed above, based on the discounted secondary market for debt, are not sufficient, creditor governments and banks could forgive the debts. Canada and a handful of European countries have already pioneered forgiveness of some debts for a few of the 'poorest' countries, but this has not become a general movement.

And, unless it is done by all major creditor governments more or less simultaneously, it will accomplish nothing for the debtor. As long as some major creditors still demand service of their debts, forgiveness by one or a few will simply force a shifting of the money which would have been paid to those creditors to the ones who do not forgive.

For at least two reasons, repudiation by the debtor is superior to forgiveness by the creditor as a means of extinguishing the debt. First, only the debtor is in a position to reduce debt service across the board to all its creditors, thus affording them equal treatment and retaining cash to spend for its own needs. Alternatively, the debtor could selectively favour some creditors – the ones in a position to do some favours in return – over others.

Second, repudiation in the face of even nominal creditor resistance requires some resolve and some willingness to act independently, and until the leadership of a debtor country is willing to stick its neck out it will not be able to undertake the other tough measures which will be necessary if it is to take advantage of its 'fresh start' to restructure its economy and discipline its spending.

The economic advantage of repudiation to the debtor countries is so obvious that knowledgeable observers are at a loss to explain why it has not happened long ago.[250] The economic benefit is equal to the cost of debt service they would not have to pay, minus the cost of sundry retaliations and harassment. It is difficult to predict the extent of the latter. The creditors find it to their advantage to exaggerate the damage they could do. Argentina was subjected to some psychological warfare in 1984, when that country threatened to defy its lenders:

> The US Treasury came up with another bit of persuasion: a list of items that would become scarce in various major debtor countries if they defaulted and imports came to a virtual standstill. . . . [The list] raised such interesting questions as: 'Have you ever contemplated what would happen to the president of a country if the government couldn't get insulin for its diabetics?'[251]

but those who have investigated the question closely believe that these threats are mostly bluff.[252]

One hypothesis is that while it is overwhelmingly to the benefit of the country as a whole to repudiate, the individuals and classes which are in control of the governments of most of the debtor countries still see their own interest as lying in obedience to the interests of creditor countries. The minister of finance who crosses the will of creditors, for example, cannot expect to get a cushy job at the IMF or World Bank when he or she leaves office, as more obedient colleagues can. Similarly, these narrowly based groups stand to benefit more from the small trickles of aid and forced lending that pass through their fingers as they come in than they pay as their share of the larger sums that go out.

The experience of Brazil, which terminated a year-long moratorium on debt service in 1988, and of Peru, which slid into chaos several years after unilaterally limiting debt payments in 1985, are often cited as proof that default hurts a country more than it harms it. No one, however, has ever shown that there was any retaliation from the banks. The man who was Finance Minister of Brazil during the moratorium dismisses the idea that there was any retaliation by the creditor banks and attributes the end of the moratorium to Brazil's domestic politics.[253] He continues to advocate a unilateral reduction of the debt, accompanied by reforms strengthening internal discipline.[254] Parallel arguments are made by students of Peru's economy: the debt policy was on balance positive for the country, but unrestrained domestic spending nullified the advantages brought by the moratorium.[255]

The economic arguments in favour of repudiation are compelling, but economic arguments are not always decisive. Behind the fears of credit cut-off and legal harassment from the banks, a deeper anxiety lurks. What will be the response of the creditor governments, and above all of the US government, to a repudiation by the debtor countries? In the late nineteenth and early twentieth centuries, gunboats were used to collect debts owed to US citizens.

Military and other forms of retaliation certainly cannot be ruled out; the precedents are numerous. But examined carefully, it can be seen that default and repudiation are at most pretexts, rather than serious reasons, for such punishment.

Zaire and Nicaragua are two extreme examples. Zairean President Mobutu Sese Seko is widely believed to be one of the most corrupt rulers of all time. The country's refusal to service its debts led the IMF to install its own man in a key position in the central bank in 1978. Anxious for a bail-out, Zaire acceded. Two years later that official, Erwin Blumenthal, resigned in frustration, reporting to the Fund that 'sordid and pernicious corruption' was so serious that 'there is no chance, I repeat no chance, that Zaire's numerous creditors will ever recover their loans.'[256] Zaire's problem was not a lack of foreign exchange, but a low priority assigned to debt service. Zaire's government preferred to use foreign exchange to feed Mobutu's overseas bank accounts, and to import luxuries.

The US government and, significantly, the IMF have shown no hostility to this defaulter. On the contrary, shortly after Blumenthal's report was received in 1981, the IMF granted Zaire what was then the largest loan ever made to an African country. As a US State Department official explained, 'it is not in our interest to contribute, directly or indirectly, to destabilization' in Zaire.[257] Although an extreme example, Zaire is not so different from many other countries which have been less than punctual in servicing their debts but which the US government does not wish to destabilise.

At the opposite extreme is the case of Nicaragua. When the Sandinistas overthrew Somoza's dictatorship in 1979 they inherited debts which included many loans incurred chiefly to purchase arms and police equipment and to pad Somoza's overseas bank accounts. After some internal debate (and, rumour has it, some advice from Fidel Castro who had repudiated the debts of his predecessor Batista) the new government decided not to repudiate the debt, negotiating instead with its creditors for better terms.

In the 1980–81 renegotiations, the new Nicaraguan government succeeded in winning the most lenient debt settlement in recent years *because* the creditors knew that repudiation was the alternative.

The Nicaraguans were eager to come to an agreement with the banks, hoping that they would avoid punitive sanctions by recognising the debt and submitting to the usual renegotiation procedures. They were to be disappointed. Bank credit was not restored, and the US sponsorship of military retaliation through their proxies the Contras demonstrates that honouring the debt is not the key to defusing hostility. Similarly, the experience of Zaire shows that failure to pay debts is not a sufficient reason for unleashing retaliation on countries that are otherwise amenable to US control.

The truth is that most of the old debt from the last debt crisis, that of the 1930s, was eventually settled at a few cents on the dollar, in part because the US government refused to intervene on behalf of the old creditors.[258] That part of the debt that was not settled was simply ignored, and not allowed to stand in the way of new business. The US Treasury continues to carry these debts on its books, and annually publishes the principal and interest owed by each of the debtor nations that defaulted in the 1930s, which include Britain, France and Italy.[259]

New creditors, including notably the US Export–Import Bank, did not wait until the defaulted debt was finally brought to a negotiated settlement, but began lending new money less than a decade after the defaults. Many of these defaults might never have been settled at all if the World Bank had not decided to act as a bill-collector, demanding compromise agreements between creditors and debtors before it would extend its own loans to the defaulting countries.[260] New creditors are not likely to be deterred by the failure to pay old debts unless they are convinced that the old creditors have the legal or political power to block their own collection of interest.[261]

24. The Asian success stories

Rather than give up capital imports, it may be argued, shouldn't indebted Third World nations strive to emulate the Asian success stories and pay off their debts with exports? It is hardly possible in this slim book to do justice to the individual complexity of even a few country case studies, but in order to evaluate this argument, let us consider the following points:

First, of the four 'little tigers' which are usually meant when Asian success stories are trotted out as models, only South Korea has been a large borrower. Singapore and Hong Kong, which as *entrepôt* cities are not typical of other Third World states, have virtually no foreign borrowing. Taiwan had some modest foreign debt during its period of tutelage under the United States but even at that time resisted US pressure to borrow and spend more freely.[262]

Taiwan began running foreign trade surpluses in 1970, exactly the point at which commercial banks were discovering the 'creditworthy' Third World and lending to finance deeper deficits. The real secret of Taiwan's quite spectacular foreign trade success is just the opposite of the one usually cited: not that it borrowed, but that it *did not borrow* during the critical years of the 1970s – when, as we argued in Chapter 16, many other Third World countries could have used high export prices to buy themselves out of their debts but instead chose to go deeper into debt. At the beginning of that decade, few observers considered Taiwan's prospects notably brighter than those of the Philippines, but it surely could have obtained bank finance if it had chosen to do so.

We are left with only South Korea, then, out of the four tigers; but one other Asian success can be added to the sample – Japan, which has made the most spectacular foreign trade turnaround from borrower (in the 1950s and 1960s) to running the largest export surplus in the world in the 1980s. The inclusion of Japan, although a developed country, is appropriate because South Korea (and Taiwan) have followed the 'Japanese model' of economic development and foreign trade policy. It is also appropriate because some analysts believe that some of the 'little tigers'' export surplus simply represents *Japanese* high-technology components, routed through electronics, shipping and automobile assembly plants in Taiwan, Korea, etc. to take advantage of the cheap labour and evade export quotas.[263]

Only one point about the 'Japanese model' need be made here: it is not at all the same model which the IMF and World Bank are foisting on their Third

World clients. The Japanese/South Korean model exhibits the *export success* which the Bank and Fund promise will be the result of adopting their conditionality, but in critical respects the *means* which Japan and South Korea have used to achieve this success run directly contrary to Fund and Bank demands.

Specifically, the demand for import and exchange liberalisation, which we have noted in previous chapters as the most fundamental aim of both IMF and World Bank Structural Adjustment conditionality, was *not* an ingredient of Japan's or of South Korea's development recipe. Imports and capital controls were 'a striking feature of foreign economic policy as well as an inseparable component of the overall growth strategy in postwar Japan'.[264] Instead, both countries followed a strategy of jealously protecting the home market and of 'surprisingly successful import substitution'.[265] Nor did either country adopt IMF-style austerity policies to restrain domestic demand. One student of Korea even concludes, 'We are certain that had Korea really followed an orthodox stabilization strategy relying on austerity, the prospects for growth would have been jeopardized.'[266]

Indeed, one source of global imbalances in the world economy in recent years has been the refusal of Japan and of Taiwan to liberalise imports, even *after* they have accumulated two of the largest hoards of foreign exchange reserves in the world, derived from many successive years of earning huge trade surpluses. South Korea has a better excuse than the others for resisting heavy US pressure to open its markets and liberalise imports, for it has made only a beginning in paying off its large foreign debt. The democratic opening in 1988 has led to consumer and worker pressures which threaten its abilities to continue to run the large surpluses for many years which will be necessary to pay off that debt.

All serious students of Japan, South Korea and Taiwan agree that state direction and control have played a major role in their industrialisation and export success, and that world market prices have played a very minor role in the organisation of their domestic economy. All these countries belie the advice of free market fanatics to 'get the prices right' after which everything else will fall into place.

To summarise, the first point which should be remembered whenever the Fund, Bank or other members of the creditors' cartel starts touting the Asian miracles as models for other debtors is that one fundamental lesson of those models is *not* to liberalise imports and thus allow foreign sellers to invade your domestic markets.[267]

The second point is perhaps even more important. That is that not everyone can win the trade surplus game. We can use the analogy of a race. If everyone running a marathon, for example, hired the best personal trainer, followed all her advice assiduously, and practised every day for a year, there would still be only one winner of the race, and no matter how fast everyone ran, there would still be one in last place.

In international trade it is of course possible for more than one country to run a surplus, but in the nature of things the global total of surpluses must equal global deficits; it is a zero-sum game. If every country tries to run a surplus at the same time, many will inevitably fail to achieve it, even if they all run draconian austerity programs and subsidise their exports to the hilt.

This is the 'fallacy of composition'. A strategy which may work when only one or a few use it, like standing on a chair to see over the heads of a crowd, can be useless if everyone tries to employ the same methods. And this failure to recognise the fallacy is a fatal flaw of the 'case by case' approach to debt problems, which tries to insist that internal policies of individual countries are responsible for a problem which can only be solved by recognising that the trade balance of any country is inevitably affected by the actions of others.

If the Latin American and African debtors all did adopt the 'Japan model' and implemented it faithfully, they would end up simply competing with each other and driving the price of their exports (whether agricultural and mineral commodities or labour-dependent manufactures) so low that only the lowest-cost countries could profitably export. Indeed, this is exactly what has happened in the 1980s. Success in increasing the quantity of exports has not been matched by a corresponding increase in export earnings, because prices have been so depressed by the competition.

And, to the extent that other debtors, such as the Latin Americans, eventually succeed in exporting to foreign markets, they would diminish the achievement of the Asian exporters.

> In reality, [South Korea's] export success, now chiefly oriented towards the American market, would have met more severe competition if the Latin American countries plus the Philippines had not been trapped in economic problems.[268]

In summary, of the so-called Asian miracles, Singapore, Hong Kong and Taiwan did not borrow. Those which did, South Korea and (in earlier decades) Japan, did not liberalise either their imports or the access of foreign direct investment to their controlled markets. All are highly dirigiste, with a complex system of state-decreed subsidies and incentives; all of which stands in stark contrast to IMF/World Bank ideology and conditionality. And their undenied success as exporters would be severely diminished if many other countries actually did adopt that model for their own economies.[269]

This brief analysis has ignored other valid critiques of the drive for export-oriented industrialisation: that the strategy assumes an expanding world market, for example (the rule about trade surpluses equalling deficits globally would hold even in an expanding market), that protectionism in the developed countries threatens to roll back export gains already made, and that the social concomitants of such a strategy, notably the repression of labour, make it undesirable in any case. Our attempt has been to show that even within its own terms, the arguments for generalisation of the 'East Asian model' do not make sense. The model does not match the reality of the societies held up as examples, and even if the model were real, it is not generalisable because world surpluses and deficits are a zero-sum game.

25. The myth of development through capital imports

Do not attempt to do us any more good. Your good has done us too much harm already.[270]

Please don't lend us any more money. Not even if we plead for another quick fix.[271]

If [foreign aid] stops, that will be the greatest service they can do us.[272]

The truism that Third World countries need foreign capital has dominated the policies of the industrial nations *and* the maldeveloped nations for decades. It is inconceivable to most people that this could not be true. Yet repeatedly, the best minds working in the field of international finance and Third World development, the people who have seen how foreign aid and loan capital have actually been used, have challenged this near-universal assumption. A distinguished economist and ex-Ambassador to India mused, rather charitably, on the origins of the belief in the saving power of foreign capital (and technology):

> What we had decided were the causes of poverty with which the Indians and we sought to contend was derived from convenience. There were, broadly speaking, only two things we could provide to lessen the deprivation – we could supply capital and, in principle, useful technical knowledge. The causes of poverty were then derived from these possibilities – poverty was seen to be the result of a shortage of capital, an absence of technical skills. The remedy included the diagnosis. Having vaccine we invented smallpox.[273]

The irony is that it is not *in spite of* but *because of* this questionable faith that foreign capital is essential to development that since 1982, the Third World has been a net *exporter* of hard currency to the developed countries, on average $30 billion per year since 1982.

Most taxpaying citizens in the West are not aware of this fact. And the experts and opinion leaders who are aware of it almost without exception deplore the situation, calling it (as we have seen) perverse, unnatural and 'bad economics'.

Yet few of those are willing to face the truth that this perverse flow is the natural, logical, and above all *legal* consequence of the very belief that foreign capital is essential to Third World development.

A few words about the meaning of 'capital' are in order here. Money is not the same thing as capital, although most of the irrationality of US foreign aid and foreign lending policy is based on the mistaken view that the two are equivalent.

Capital is a term for assets, whether in the form of money or otherwise, which are used for the purpose of making more money. Land may be capital if it is exploited for the purpose of making money. Factory machinery is capital. So are inventories of raw materials and the products of the factories. Capital may be embodied in many forms, but it is capital *only* if it is employed in the quest for more money. Money which is used for consumption or any other purpose is not capital. And even money that is employed in the quest for more money does not necessarily result in the creation of real productive assets, as many critiques of the current US economy have pointed out.

Joan Robinson ridiculed the confusion of money with capital in neoclassical economics by labelling it 'putty-capital'.

> Capital consists of lumps of putty and the rate of interest is determined by the ratio of putty-capital to labour, being equal to marginal productivity of putty.
>
> In this scheme of ideas, international capital flows consist of exports of putty from one country to another. A rich, high-wage country had a high putty–labour ratio and a low rate of interest. Therefore it exports its putty-savings to a country with a higher rate of interest. Savings of putty, it seems, are put on a boat and sent to be used as putty-capital in the low-wage country.
>
> Now, it is true that 'capital', in the sense of capital goods, say steel ingots or machine-tools, may be put onto a ship and sent from one country to another, but this is not necessarily associated with a movement of 'capital' in the sense of finance, for the goods may be paid for by visible or invisible exports going in the opposite direction. On the other hand, finance may pass from one country to another to be expended exclusively in employing labour and buying property on the spot, so there is no movement of capital goods. *A country which receives an inflow of finance is not receiving a supply of a factor of production called 'capital,' it is enjoying the possibility of running a surplus of imports or amassing monetary reserves.*[274]

Not all money shipped abroad, as foreign aid or commercial lending, is employed in productive investment so that it could earn the name of capital. Even when money is apparently invested, it may not be wisely or prudently invested. And even when investment is based on sober calculation and not diluted by fraud, kickbacks or 'skimming' of payments, the highly unstable international economic conditions which have been the norm for at least the past two decades may make a hash of the best calculations.

The structure of our argument to this point has slighted the question of what the borrowed money actually purchased. Anyone familiar with the real world of foreign aid and foreign lending knows that there is a tremendous amount of waste and fraud involved (some of which shows up in the imputed calculations of capital flight). Other uses of the money, which do not fall into the categories of outright waste or theft, include general imports to keep inflation low and the population happy; armaments for prosecuting foreign wars or suppressing the domestic population; prestige projects which do not earn income; investment in local production which does not earn foreign exchange; etc. We have seen that as the debt burden mounts, an increasing proportion of borrowing has to be used to pay service on the old debt, and so is not available as productive capital or for any other use. But the economy as a whole has to pay for the interest on *all* foreign borrowing, no matter how it was used.

The truly scarce commodity in the world today is not capital; it is markets. If you doubt the truth of this statement, read the business page of your local newspaper[275] for the latest diatribe by US business or government against the Japanese, the Europeans, South Korea, Taiwan, Brazil or Mexico. You will never find a complaint that they are competing with the United States for capital (indeed, most are supplying it to the United States). You will find that the United States is whining for one of two reasons: 1. They are committing 'unfair' trade practices by exporting cheaper or better commodities to the United States, or 2. They are not buying as much of US exports as the United States would like to sell them.

The aid and credit business is a cleverly designed tool to bribe nations with money to give the creditors or aid donors access to the home market of the recipient. So-called 'tied aid' is one way in which this is done. Credit is extended by an aid agency not in the form of money, but only for the purchase of goods produced in one country, and typically available only for those goods in which that country is not fully competitive internationally. The terms of aid are finely adjusted to compensate for the overpricing via-a-vis competitors. Even the formally 'untied' bank loans of the 1970s were frequently *de facto* made conditional on the recipient country or corporation awarding the business to a corporation from the country lending the money.[276]

The use of credit to pry markets open is also obvious in the 'conditionality' of the IMF and the World Bank. The *sine qua non* of conditions required by these organisations is import liberalisation; all the other conditions are subsidiary to that primary demand. Import liberalisation means the dismantlement, at least partially, of trade barriers, whether these be exchange controls, import bans, quotas, lowering of tariffs or any other policy which prevents corporations from the industrialised countries from selling as much as they wish. It represents the surrender of all or part of the domestic market to foreign sellers and is, incidentally, about the worst possible policy that can be imagined for any country short of capital. But to the sellers, credit is considered a cheap way to buy markets.

While cavilling and grumbling about all other types of aid programs,

Congress has consistently proved to be exceptionally eager to fund the Export–Import bank, because this is recognised to be a direct, foolproof way to fund US exports to the rest of the world. The bilateral foreign aid program has been called 'the soft-loan window of the Export–Import Bank', by a US Senator who added:

> [I]t is the source from which foreign governments borrow money on easy terms with which to buy goods and services from within the United States. As such, it enjoys a lively constituency which exerts steady pressure on the Government to keep the program going.[277]

Conversely, the type of aid most bitterly opposed has been that which is suspected of funding exports which would compete with those of 'our' producers (World Bank projects are occasionally attacked in Congress for this reason).[278]

It is an open secret that practically all aid agencies, from the World Bank to small bilateral programs, have a 'disbursement problem'. A disbursement (or absorption) problem is shorthand for the fact that aid agencies cannot identify enough attractive projects to absorb the funds they are obliged to disburse within a given time period.

Where then, does the idea come from that the Third World is short of capital? It comes largely from macroeconomic models constructed in air-conditioned offices in Washington, London, Paris and other capitals far from the realities on the ground in the Third World. If one takes a hypothetical target growth rate, then adds an assumed 'capital–output ratio' it is a simple, but sterile, academic exercise to calculate the amount of capital that would be needed to achieve the target growth rate. These estimates are then used as the basis for pledging at the next meeting of the aid consortium.

Such models encourage the illusion that infusions of money, for almost any purpose, will aid 'growth'.

> [I]f external resources are assumed to be the limiting factor, any particular infusion of such resources is presumed to help. This means that the particular investment to be aided is not subject to any very rigorous test.[279]

It is left to the aid officials on the ground to figure out how to pour tons of liquidity into economies that can profitably absorb only quarts or gallons – without wasting the amounts that can't be absorbed. Of course it can't be done, and something has to give. Either the money is 'wasted' on projects whose profitability has been exaggerated by doctored cost–benefit exercises, or it is siphoned into the pockets of recipient country officials who have an obvious pecuniary interest in not revealing that it cannot be profitably invested. In the most honest agencies it remains unspent.[280]

Although we are told that Africa is not getting enough cash, harassed aid

> administrators in the field often compete with each other to spend their dollars and search in vain for worthwhile projects to fund. Money ostentatiously committed by their governments frequently remains unspent at the end of the financial year.[281]

Sometimes the waste takes obvious forms: Mexico and Venezuela are the champions of capital flight, with Argentina, Brazil, Nigeria and the Philippines as runners-up.[282] Debt incurred for the purpose of arms imports has been estimated as amounting to 15 per cent of the total of all Third World debt contracted between 1972 and 1982; the major offenders here include Egypt and several other Middle Eastern countries but also India, Pakistan, Korea and Indonesia in Asia, Algeria, Morocco and Nigeria in Africa, and Argentina, Chile and Peru in South America.[283] Waste also takes the form of swelling imports for consumption or for nonproductive investment.

The solution, then, we are complacently instructed, is to invest the money productively and not wastefully. The big mistake of the Latin debtors was that they did not do that. It sounds so easy. But only a few analysts perceived the waste while it was happening. Most have discerned it only with twenty-twenty hindsight, after the debt crisis broke and 'proved' that in fact, the money had not be productively invested.

In fact, discerning in advance (as *all* investment decisions must be made) what will turn out to be a productive or a profitable investment is a difficult exercise. Three-quarters of US small businesses, and not a few of the largest, fail; how can we expect omniscience of Third World entrepreneurs, private or public? When the money was spent, most of the players concerned thought that it was going for productive investment; and if they knew better, they kept quiet. Even some countries which were investing productively got caught in the debt trap. Brazil, Chile and the Philippines are three countries whose investment projects were – at the time they could still borrow – viewed approvingly by nearly everyone who knew anything about them.

> The overwhelming majority of the borrowing went, directly or indirectly, to boost production of basic industrial products. In principle, the system was magical: foreign finance boosted industrial production, and enough of this production was exported to cover interest and principal payments.[284]
>
> In several cases, of which Chile and Brazil are only the most obvious examples, the borrowers' economic policies were actively encouraged by the United States and other creditor governments.[285]
>
> One of Virata's staff offered an explanation: 'Sure, we're up to our eyeballs in debt, but to "take off" you have to spend.' That was a 'basic economic law,' said the Central Bank's Zialcita. . . . To paraphrase top Philippine technocrats, the dollar amount of external debt was irrelevant, for the loans were being channeled into productive export-oriented industrialization.[286]

But 'productive' is not the same thing as 'profitable'. That is, many so-called productive projects were built with insufficient attention to the critical business relationship between costs of production and availability of markets at a price that would cover those costs. One thoughtful analyst of the Sicartsa project, a 'productive' steel mill in Mexico, discovered a veritable horror story of incompetence and indifference on the part of those financing the plant, which became a famous failure.

> Few players carefully analysed the economics of the mill. Participating banks relied on lead banks, who in turn relied on the exporters for the analysis. . . . Exporters appeared to have relied on the buyer. The same is true of the official lenders: Britain's aid agency had no time for on-site inspection and the others did not make them. Even builders who objected to the mill – as being the wrong type, for example – bid anyway.
>
> Sicartsa suggests that several G-5 [Group of Five: United States, United Kingdom, Germany, France, Japan] governments actively pushed credit onto Mexico for a bad project and encouraged their banks to lend to the same end. Sicartsa may be one of the largest . . . but it is not an isolated case.[287]

There are many possible slip-ups between the borrowing to construct a 'productive' project and the eventual triumphant ability to service, and eventually repay, the money which was borrowed.

First, the project must not be only productive, but profitable, a more severe criterion, or no one will want its production, and in fact it will be wasted money.

Second, if foreign exchange must be repaid, the project must be not just profitable in the domestic context but profitable, or competitive, in the export market.

Too many projects, like Sicartsa, did not meet even the first test. But many did. And here we arrive at the crushing irony of the borrowing for productive projects.

The productive, profitable, hard-currency-earning plants must earn enough not only to service their own borrowing, but to pay as well for all the borrowing for all the nonexporting, nonprofitable, nonproductive, and downright wasteful projects that went on that country's bill during its borrowing binge.

> Even foreign loans for specific productive purposes can hurt an economy. If the local government could have financed a good project without the foreign loan, one effect of a foreign loan would be to free up funds for the government to use. One must examine not merely the project itself, but government expenditures at the margin, in order to weigh the effects of the foreign loan.[288]
>
> It soon became recognised . . . that foreign capital was financing not the project to which it apparently was tied but the marginal investment project, i.e. of all those projects undertaken, the one that ranked lowest on a list of priorities. Thus aid was financing not the most attractive but the least

attractive, or marginal, project. This is what is meant . . . when it is said that aid is 'fungible'.

There is no reason to stop at this point, however . . . foreign capital finances not the marginal investment project but the marginal *expenditure* project, and expenditure on the margin is just as likely (perhaps more likely) to be on consumption goods as on capital goods.[289]

In a series of elegant and forceful articles, the economist Keith Griffin has spelled out the arguments against foreign aid. We have dealt with his criticisms of the dominant theoretical models justifying foreign capital flows in Chapter 6. He also spells out the conditions under which foreign capital borrowing is economically justified:

Assuming that a country invests a certain fraction of its net capital inflow, foreign capital will raise total output to an amount equal to the amount *actually invested* times the incremental output–capital ratio [a tautological ratio beloved of economists that simply measures the productivity of capital on new investments in that economy]. *Interest, however, must be paid on the entire loan, not just on that part which is invested.* If the product of that fraction of imported capital which is actually invested is less than the interest due on the *entire amount* of borrowed capital, the additional output generated by the imported capital will be insufficient to service the debt.[290] Either the country will be unable to pay the debt, or it will have to allocate the product of its domestically generated invested savings to debt service (living below its means), or it will have to borrow more from abroad, if that is still a viable option in the short term.

In brief, this means that in order for an economy to be able to service its foreign debts, its productive investments must be so fabulously profitable *in international markets* that they are able to carry the interest on all the borrowed foreign exchange that is spent on military purchases, all the funds that escape the country as capital flight, all the 'unproductive' consumption imports, and all the projects which did not achieve the critical level of international competitiveness. It is a heroic achievement; of the current borrowers, only one, South Korea, is in sight of fulfilling these demanding conditions (and the popular demands stimulated by its 1988 democratisation may yet reverse that trend). And historically, 'Only in the case of the United States and the British dominions, *despite substantial waste*, were productive investments undertaken that led to substantial economic growth.'[291]

But it is even worse. Not only does imported capital, whatever it is used for, require debt service which must be covered by that portion of it that is profitably invested; the conditions attached by the creditors for the use of that aid limit the possibility of its profitable investment.

First, the practice of aid-tying means that borrowers are not able to obtain the best price for the goods they purchase, but are constrained to take overpriced goods for which credit is available from the producers and their export finance agencies. Goods that are competitive internationally, that is, that can obtain orders because of price and/or quality without credit, are almost never available on credit financing. Aid-financed goods also tend to generate a continuing demand for spare parts and inputs which are only available from one source and at a non competitive price, thus adding to the foreign-exchange drain.

Second, aid agencies have definite ideological biases against government ownership of directly productive activities, which leads to a bias in favour of infrastructure, social overhead, and, increasingly, financing consumption imports – none of which are directly productive.[292] At the same time both official and private creditors insist on *de jure* or *de facto* government guarantees for all their lending, leaving the government with all the responsibility and few of the resources for servicing the debt.

Third, if aid or capital flows are conditioned on the adoption of IMF and World Bank conditionality, opportunities for the profitable investment of capital will be severely constrained by the effects of that conditionality. Specifically, domestic producers are handicapped by the competition they meet from imports financed by the credits and to which the door has been thrown open by the import liberalisation always demanded by the Fund and Bank.

> Most of the countries we would wish to assist would not be helped by cuts in our imports from them, or by expanding those of our exports to them which compete with their domestic industries.[293]

In theory, and to a certain extent in practice, exporters benefit from these policies, e.g. devaluation of the national currency. The experience of the world's most successful exporters (Japan, Taiwan, South Korea) suggests, however, that export success is founded on a protected domestic market and is not dependent, as the IMF and World Bank contend, on the destruction of that market.

Finally (and this criticism should be understood by the ardent advocates of unfettered market relationships), inflows of public or private capital distort price relations within a country and between that country and the rest of the world. Capital flows are a type of subsidy which provide a price advantage to imported goods unrelated to their actual costs of production and therefore handicap locally competing goods, as we have already mentioned. But the distorting effects of capital flows are society-wide.

> Large entries of capital in response to interest rate differentials may sustain exchange rates that prejudice the development of sustainable export capacity, and hence the ability eventually to repay debt.[294]
>
> Governing elites allow exchange rates to become grossly overvalued. This then presents the financial elites (often the same people) with a one-way bet on the direction of future exchange rate movements. A more sensible exchange rate policy would stop this speculative activity, help to reduce capital flight, discourage cheap imports from abroad at the expense of domestic industry and help to encourage exports. The exchange rate is one price that governments should 'get right'.[295]

It is of course always possible to disregard these theoretical caveats about productive investment and build 'cash-flow' models of the gap between projected inflow and projected outflow. In the post-1982 world it is simple to find a horrendous 'foreign exchange gap' by calculating projected export earnings, projected (i.e. desired) import expenditures, and adding this to the large negative net transfer (payments on debt service minus new inflows of capital) which by itself practically guarantees a gap. Those who construct these cash-flow models seldom stop to question why export earnings are so abysmally low,[296] why inessential imports should not be banned in the national interest,[297] and why the imperative to *import* foreign capital has paradoxically resulted in a situation where the borrowers are compelled to *export* foreign exchange. But until we ask those questions, and find the answers, we will not solve the debt crisis.

26. Avoiding the next crisis

It is probably as useless to try to ban credit as it is to try to ban alcohol or the other drugs which give unhappy humans a temporary high. There are still some legitimate uses for credit, and there will never be agreement on where the legitimate uses shade off into the illegitimate, just as we cannot agree on exactly how to indulge in harmless social drinking without risking alcoholism.

Nevertheless, there are dangers in credit, just as there are in alcohol and drugs, and, contrary to popular belief, the dangers that innocent victims will be hurt is far greater when nations are borrowing than when persons or corporations borrow. The problem is not simply one of generations, although that alone would be a sufficient reason not to borrow. The real problem is that those who have to bear the heavy cost of repaying the loans with interest are not the same people who benefited from the loans, and are not even the children of those who benefited in most cases.

Foreign borrowing allows corruption, the theft from the public purse, which seems to be endemic to most political systems, to exceed even the amounts which are gathered in by taxation each year. Those who have 'sacked' the public credit (those who engage in capital flight are called *saqueros* in Spanish) can rob from the state, from the tax coffers, not only the receipts of the public budget of this year, but the receipts of many years to come – an infinity of years, if the debts are not repudiated.

And there is the political danger – which has become a desperate reality in the 1980s – that the real sovereignty of the nation will be handed over to foreign creditors and their governments. And while private creditors have the interest of draining money from the debtor's carcase, creditor governments wish to substitute their own priorities for those of the leaders chosen by the citizens of the debtor nations.

Recognising that good advice is powerless in the face of enormous monetary incentives such as easy borrowing (for the debtors) and quick profits (for the lenders) we will nevertheless try in this last chapter to suggest guidelines for foreign borrowing in the future.

First, the ideal should not be long-term lopsided borrowing, with countries divided into semi-permanent creditors and semi-permanent debtors, but should aim at balance, not necessarily within the limits of only one year but certainly over the short term. The idea that some countries are 'natural' importers of capital over a long period of time must be discarded. Devotees of international comparative advantage should ponder the fact that only under a regime of balanced, two-way trade can true comparative advantage be ascertained; unbalanced capital flows by definition distort price relationships.

Would this doom the poor nations to stagnation? Just the opposite. One of the suppressed stories of the past century is the fact that development, and structural change, proceeded faster and more satisfactorily throughout the Third World during the period of the Great Depression than in the period when international loans were easy to obtain.[298] Necessity is the mother of invention, and of import substitution.

Second, foreign borrowing for consumption is legitimate only in emergency situations, such as a catastrophic and widespread harvest failure, and if the 'emergency' persists for more than one year it should be treated as if it had become a permanent condition. Much overborrowing is due to the failure to recognise that an adverse change in economic conditions may be more than just temporary. Foreign borrowing should *never* be used to make up a government budget deficit or to support the exchange rate, except to smooth out *very* short-term fluctuations.

Third, foreign creditors should eschew the temptation to impose conditions on the uses of their loans or to hide behind IMF or World Bank conditionality. This might seem to fly in the face of prudence, as well as normal lending practice. It follows naturally, however, from what we have said in the previous chapter about foreign borrowing financing the marginal expenditure project; as money is fungible, creditors only fool themselves if they believe they can control its uses. And conditions imposed by outsiders far from the site of the investment usually do more harm than good.

Fourth, citizens of the borrowing country, on the other hand, should take seriously the duty of monitoring the uses of and accounting for foreign loans. They should debate the social utility of each loan before it is entered on the register. Creditors must honour this duty by countenancing the repudiation of loans that are contracted in violation of the laws of the borrowing country. Their behaviour in the present crisis has been exactly the opposite: they have forced national governments to assume responsibility for private debts which were never officially guaranteed.

Fifth, when loans go sour, creditors must swallow their losses. This is axiomatic within the US domestic context; bankruptcy law recognises the desirability, from the point of view of the economy as a whole, of wiping bad debts off the books and giving the debtor a 'fresh start'.[299] But the major difference between the current debt crisis and previous international defaults is that this principle has been disparaged by the major creditors, whose home governments have supported them.

Finally, since it is probably futile to think we can banish foreign borrowing from the world, we might adopt another domestic practice, that of registering international claims on some official and *public* list, analogous to local mortgage registers. The World Bank has heretofore done a very poor job of monitoring and limiting foreign debt exposure; it might find a positive function in sponsoring this official registry (but would have to accept the passive role of clerk; no conditionality permitted). The advantages of such a registry are several:

- Creditors whose loans were not publicly registered would have no legal claim on a country's foreign exchange earnings. *This must be strictly enforced.* The failure to do this has nullified previous efforts to register foreign debts, and led to situations in which, when the debt crisis breaks, no one at all has any idea how big the debt burden actually is. This would also preclude creditors from ganging up to force governments to assume the burden of paying unguaranteed and unsecured private debts.
- As the registry is public, no one could make secret deals pledging future public revenues.
- New creditors would have an accurate picture of the other claims on a country's future earnings. This function would be enhanced if the country involved also set a legal limit on the amount of debt service payable in any given period.
- In case the amount of debt service due on registered debt exceeded the legal limit payable, the registry would establish automatic priorities for debt service. The priorities should be arbitrarily set, with no room for subjective judgment about the social value of any particular loan, which would open the door to politicking and other abuses. My own preference is for chronological priorities: the first loans registered would be paid in full; the most recent would receive nothing. Such a rule would reward the first lenders for resuming credit to a country which had trouble getting credit and, if enforced, would effectively preclude the speculative lending by latecomers which caused the most problems in the current debt cycle.

If adopted and enforced, these rules should be quite effective in preventing overborrowing, and, if it occurs, in limiting the debt service burden to the country while penalising precisely the lenders responsible for the over-borrowing. They are not designed to encourage creditors to resume lending to the Third World (just the contrary), but do allow it within limits of prudence.

'Neither a borrower nor a lender be,' advised Shakespeare, who also warned, in a different play, about the Pound of Flesh. 'For loan oft loses both itself and friend, and borrowing dulls the edge of husbandry.' It would be difficult to summarise the message of this book more succinctly.

Notes and references

Introduction

1. E.g. James P. Grant, *The State of the World's Children 1989* (New York: Oxford University Press for UNICEF, 1989); Susan George, *A Fate Worse Than Debt* (New York: Grove Press, 1988).

2. On the relationship of Canada's foreign debt and that of the Third World, see 'Canada's indebtedness', Chapter 6 of the excellent study by GATT–Fly, *Debt Bondage or Self-Reliance* (Toronto: GATT–Fly, 1985 and supplements). This is one of the best single studies of the Third World debt crisis.

3. See the series of country aid studies and Norwegian aid reviews published by the Christian Michelsen Institute of Bergen and the Centre for Development Studies of the University of Bergen for specific examples of aid objectives distorted by the needs of Norwegian exporters and Norwegian consultant firms familiar only with technology produced by other Norwegian businesses.

Chapter 1

4. Harold Lever and Christopher Huhne, *Debt and Danger: The World Financial Crisis* (Harmondsworth: Penguin, 1985) pp. 11–12. My emphasis.

5. Organisation for Economic Cooperation and Development, *Twenty-Five Years of Development Cooperation* (Paris: OECD, 1985) p. 159. My emphasis.

6. Henry Bittermann, *The Refunding of International Debt* (Durham, N.C.: Duke University Press, 1973) pp. 5, 17. My emphasis.

7. Jane Sueddon Little, *Eurodollars: The Money-Market Gypsies*, (New York: Harper & Row, 1975) p. 120.

8. Keith Griffin, *Underdevelopment in Spanish America: an interpretation* (London: Allen & Unwin, 1969) pp. 242–3.

9. Source of graph: Charles R. Frank, Jr., 'Debt and Terms of Aid', in Overseas Development Council, *Assisting Developing Countries* (New York: Praeger, 1972) p. 31.

10. James P. Grant (President of the Overseas Development Council) in Overseas Development Council, *New Directions in Development* (New York, Praeger, 1974).

11. Rehman Sobhan, *The Crisis of External Dependence: The Political Economy of Foreign Aid to Bangladesh* (London: Zed Press, 1982) pp. 45–56.

12. For example, the first loan ever made by the World Bank, to France in 1946, was held up until assurances were received that the Communist Party would be excluded from a coalition government (Walter Issacson, *The Wise Men: Six Friends and the World They Made: Acheson, Bohlen, Harriman, Kennan, Lovett, McCloy* (New York: Simon and Schuster, 1986) p. 429. Even thirty years later, economic

assistance from the IMF and the EEC to Italy was manipulated for the same purpose – to preclude Communist Party membership in a coalition government. Cheryl Payer, 'The Politics of Intervention: The Italian Crisis of 1976' in Stephen Resnick and Richard Wolff, *Rethinking Marxism* (Brooklyn: Autonomedia, 1985).

13. See Chapter 18 for details; also see my books on the IMF and World Bank. Cheryl Payer, *The Debt Trap: The IMF and the Third World* (Harmondsworth: Penguin, 1974 and New York: Monthly Review, 1975) and Payer, *The World Bank: A Critical Analysis* (New York: Monthly Review, 1982).

14. For an elaboration of this argument, see Alfred J. Watkins, *Till Debt Do Us Part: Who wins, Who loses, and who pays, for the international debt crisis* (Washington: Roosevelt Center for American Policy Studies, 1986).

Chapter 2

15. S. C. Gwynne, *Selling Money* (New York: Penguin, 1986) p. 65.

16. Organisation for Economic Cooperation and Development, *Debt Problems of Developing Countries* (Paris: OECD, 1974) para. 41, p. 14.

17. Rosario Green, *El endeudamiento publico externo de Mexico, 1940–1973* (Mexico: El Colegio de Mexico, 1976) p. 113.

18. A good early discussion of the problems with using this single ratio can be found in Dragoslav Avramović *et al.*, *Economic Growth and External Debt* (Baltimore: Johns Hopkins Press for IBRD, 1960) Chapter IV.

19. World Bank, *World Debt Tables, 1988–89 Edition*, vol. 1: Analysis and Summary Tables, p. 20.

20. Aldo Ferrer, *Living Within Our Means* (Boulder: Westview Press, 1985).

Chapter 3

21. *New York Times*, 7 December 1986; C. P. Kindleberger, *Manias, Panics, and Crashes: A History of Financial Crises* (New York: Basic Books, 1978) pp. 85–6.

22. Organisation for Economic Cooperation and Development, *Debt Problems of Developing Countries* (Paris: OECD, 1974) para. 45. Emphasis in original.

23. Dragoslav Avramović, *et al.*, *Economic Growth and External Debt* (Baltimore: Johns Hopkins University Press for the World Bank, 1964) tables 3.1 and 3.2.

24. Harry Magdoff, *The Age of Imperialism* (New York: Monthly Review Press, 1969) p. 153 and table XXXII.

25. Henry Bittermann, *op. cit.*, Appendix, pp. 244–50.

Chapter 4

26. I owe this insight to a conversation with Arthur Goldschmidt on 18 November 1986.

27. Randall Hinshaw, 'Foreign Investment and American Employment', Papers and Proceedings of the 58th Annual Meeting of the American Economic Association, 24–27 January 1946, *American Economic Review*, p. 662.

28. Hal B. Lary, 'The Domestic Effects of Foreign Investment', *ibid.*, p. 678.

29. Randolph E. Paul, *Taxation for Prosperity* (Indianapolis: Bobbs-Merrill, 1947) p. 248. My emphasis.

30. Susan Strange, 'Protectionism and World Politics', *International Organization* **39**, 2 (1985) pp. 239–40.

31. John Maynard Keynes, *Collected Writings*, vol. XXI, (London: Macmillan) p. 59.

32. Hinshaw, p. 664.

33. Hinshaw, pp. 665–6. My emphasis.
34. National Planning Association, *New Opportunities in World Trade* (November 1944) p. 18.
35. Lary, p. 683. My emphasis.
36. Paul, *loc. cit.*
37. Jacob Viner, 'International Finance in the Postwar World', *The Journal of Political Economy* **55** (April 1947), p. 106.
38. E. D. Domar, 'The Effect of Foreign Investment on the Balance of Payments', *American Economic Review* **40** (December 1950) pp. 805–25.
39. *Report to the President on Foreign Economic Policies* (Washington, 10 November 1950) pp. 63–4.

Chapter 5

40. Colin Clark, 'The World Will Save Money in the 1950s', *Fortune*, July 1950, p. 89.
41. *op. cit.*, p. 89.
42. *ibid*, p. 124. My emphasis.
43. *ibid.*, p. 128.
44. *loc. cit.*

Chapter 6

45. E. Phelps Brown, 'The Underdevelopment of Economics', (Presidential address to the Royal Economic Society, 8 July 1971) *Economic Journal* **82**, pp. 1–10 (March 1972) p. 2.
46. Wassily Leontief, 'Theoretical Assumptions and Nonobserved Facts', Presidential Address, *American Economic Review* **56**, 1 (1971) p. 2.
47. Paul Rosenstein-Rodan, 'International Aid for Underdeveloped Countries', *Review of Economics and Statistics* Vol. 43 (1961), pp. 107–38.
48. *ibid.*, p. 107.
49. *ibid.*, p. 108.
50. *ibid.*, p. 109.
51. *ibid.*, p. 109.
52. From W. W. Rostow, *The Stages of Economic Growth, A Non-Communist Manifesto* (Cambridge University Press, 1960).
53. Dragoslav Avramović *et al.*, *Economic Growth and External Debt* (Baltimore: Johns Hopkins Press for the IBRD, 1964) p. 193. My emphasis.
54. Raymond Mikesell, *The Economics of Foreign Aid and Self-Sustaining Development* (Boulder: Westview, 1983) p. 55.
55. H. B. Chenery and Alan Strout, 'Foreign Assistance and Economic Development', *American Economic Review* **56** (1966) pp. 680–733.
56. *ibid.*, p. 679.
57. H. B. Chenery, 'Objectives and Criteria of Foreign Assistance', in *The United States and the Developing Economies*, ed. G. Ranis (New York: W. W. Norton, 1964) p. 81.
58. *ibid.*, pp. 682, 697–700.
59. I. M. D. Little, Tibor Scitavsky and Maurice Scott, *Industry and Trade in Some Developing Countries: A Comparative Study* (London and New York: Oxford University Press for the OECD Development Centre, 1970); Bela Balassa, *Development Strategies in Some Developing Countries: A Comparative Study*

(Baltimore: Johns Hopkins University Press for the World Bank, 1971); Jagdish Bhagwati, *Anatomy and Consequences of Exchange Control Regimes* (Cambridge: Ballinger, for the National Bureau of Economic Research, 1978); Anne Krueger, *Foreign Trade Regimes and Economic Development: Liberalization Attempts and Consequences* (New York: National Bureau of Economic Research, 1978) are the cover volumes. Many of the country case studies were published separately.

60. Albert O. Hirschman, *Essays in Trespassing*, (Cambridge University Press, 1981), pp. 113, 114–15.

61. K. B. Griffin and J. L. Enos, 'Foreign Assistance: Objectives and Consequences', *Economic Development and Cultural Change* **18** (1970) pp. 313–27; Keith Griffin, *International Inequality and National Poverty* (London: Macmillan, 1978) Chapter 3: 'Foreign capital, domestic savings, and economic development'; Keith Griffin, 'Doubts About Aid', *IDS Bulletin* **17** (1986), pp. 36–45; Heinrich Bortis, *Foreign Resources and Economic Development from the Early Fifties to the Oil Crisis*, Institut des Sciences Economiques et Sociales de L'Université de Fribourg, Documents économiques no. 11 (Fribourg Suisse, Editions Universitaires, 1979).

62. Griffin and Enos, 'Foreign Assistance', pp. 319–20.

63. Griffin and Enos, 'Foreign Assistance', p. 321, quoting H. B. Chenery, 'Trade, Aid, and Economic Development', in *International Development 1965*, ed. S. H. Robock and L. M. Soloman (Dobbs Ferry, N.Y.: Oceana Publications, 1966) p. 187.

64. Griffin, 'Foreign capital', p. 61.

65. See, for example, his handbook for revolutionary change: Keith Griffin and Jeffrey James, *The Transition to Equalitarian Development* (London: Macmillan, 1980).

66. *ibid.*, p. 685, note 10. My emphasis.

Chapter 7

67. S. C. Gwynne, *Selling Money* (New York: Penguin, 1986) p. 65.

68. Douglass C. North, 'International Capital Movements in Historical Perspective', in Raymond Mikesell, ed., *U.S. Private and Government Investment Abroad* (Eugene: University of Oregon Press, 1962) p. 32.

69. Although this is frequently confused with Rostow's 'stages of economic growth', this is analytically separate and predates Rostow's work.

70. Dragoslav Avramović, who kindly read an earlier draft of this work, has pointed out that credit expansion to accommodate this expenditure is a necessary condition of this scenario.

71. Paul Samuelson, *Economics*, 10th Edition (New York: McGraw Hill, 1976) pp. 660–1.

72. Charles J. Bullock, John H. Williams and Rufus S. Tucker, 'The Balance of Trade of the United States', *The Review of Economic Statistics*, **1** (1919) part I.

73. Compare Keynes' remarks, *supra*, p. 20.

74. In 1988, the United States again became a net debtor nation, as its payments to foreign owners of US assets exceeded foreign payments to US owners of foreign assets. Samuelson has no label for this stage!

75. D. C. M. Platt, *Foreign Finance in Continental Europe and the United States, 1815–1870* (London: George Allen & Unwin, 1984) pp. 183–4.

76. Bullock, Williams and Tucker, p. 224.

77. Some of these thoughts were inspired by Robert Solomon, 'The United States as a Debtor in the 19th Century', Brookings Discussion Papers in International

Economics, **28** (May 1985).

78. Ole David Koht Norbye, 'The International Debt Burden in Norway, 1865–1985', unpublished draft, 5 March 1987, p. 11.

79. K. E. Berrill, 'Foreign Capital and Take-off' in W. W. Rostow, ed. *The Economics of Take-Off into Sustained Growth* (New York: St. Martin's Press, 1963) p. 295.

80. W. W. Rostow, *Eisenhower, Kennedy, and Foreign Aid*, (Austin: University of Texas Press, 1985) p. 129.

81. Platt, *op. cit.*, p. 184.

82. An analysis of the Asian 'success stories' can be found in Chapter 24.

Chapter 8

83. Stephany Griffith-Jones, *Transnational Finance and Latin American National Development*, IDS Working Paper **175** 1982, p.3.

84. *ibid.*, p.3.

85. *ibid.*, p.8.

86. *ibid.*, p.14.

87. *Banking*, August 1950, p.122. My emphasis.

88. The linguistic use of 'capital' as a substitute for money is so pervasive that it would be awkward to find another for this text. This convention, and the assumptions behind it will be criticised in Chapter 25, however.

89. The statistical categories recognised by OECD are as follows:

I. Official Development Assistance
  A. Flows from bilateral sources
    1. DAC [developed capitalist countries: members of the Development Advisory Committee of the OECD]
    2. OPEC [members of the Organization of Petroleum Exporting Countries]
    3. CMEA [Soviet bloc: members of the Council of Mutual Economic Assistance or Comecon]
    4. Non-DAC/OECD
    5. LDC [less developed country] donors
  B. Flows from multilateral agencies [IMF, World Bank, regional development banks, etc.]
II. Grants by private voluntary agencies
III. Non-concessional flows
  A. Official or officially supported
    1. Private export credits (DAC)
    2. Official export credits (DAC)
    3. Multilateral
    4. Other official and private flows (DAC)
    5. Other donors
  B. Private
    1. Direct investment
    2. Bank sector
    3. Bond lending

Chapter 9

90. Russell Edgerton, 'The Creation of the Development Loan Fund', PhD thesis, Colombia University, 1967, p.9.

91. Walt Whitman Rostow, *Eisenhower, Kennedy, and Foreign Aid* (Austin: University of Texas Press, 1985) p.263.
92. *ibid.*, p.96.
93. Office of Strategic Services, the wartime precursor of the Central Intelligence Agency.
94. Edgerton, p.93.
95. Edgerton, p.100.
96. Max Millikan and Walt Whitman Rostow, *A Proposal: Keys to An Effective Foreign Policy* (New York: Harper, 1957).
97. *ibid.*, p.82. My emphasis.
98. *ibid.*, p.84.
99. *ibid.*, p.85.
100. *ibid.*, p.158.
101. Max Millikan and Donald Blackmer, ed., *The Emerging Nations: Their Growth and United States Policy* (Boston: Little, Brown and Company, 1961) pp.x–xi.
102. *ibid.*, pp.118–19.

Chapter 10

103. Alvin Hansen, *Economic Issues of the 1960s* (New York: McGraw-Hill, 1960) pp.127–8. Emphasis mine.
104. John Foster Dulles announcing the establishment of the Development Loan Fund in 1957, quoted in W. W. Rostow, *Eisenhower, Kennedy, and Foreign Aid* (Austin: University of Texas Press, 1985) p.129.
105. Edgerton, pp.81–2.
106. Quoted in Edgerton, p.35. My emphasis.
107. Edgerton, p.36.
108. Barbara R. Berman, comment on Wilson Schmidt, 'Default of International Public Debts', *The National Banking Review* **2**: 403–5 (1965). Comment by Berman and reply by Schmidt (who concurred with the quoted sentence) in *ibid.*, **2**: 569–71 (1965).
109. Dragoslav Avramović and Ravi Gulhati, *Debt Servicing Problems of Low-Income Countries 1956–58* (Baltimore: Johns Hopkins Press for the IBRD, 1960) p.56.
110. *ibid.*, p.59.
111. Charles R. Frank, 'Debt and Terms of Aid', in Overseas Development Council, *Assisting Developing Countries* (New York: Praeger, 1972) p.34.
112. Poul Høst-Madsen, 'What does it mean: a deficit in the balance of payments?' *Finance and Development* **3**:174 (1966).

Chapter 11

113. Jerome Levinson and Juan de Onis, *The Alliance That Lost Its Way: a critical report on the Alliance for Progress* (Chicago: Quadrangle Books, 1970) p.138.
114. William T. Denzer, Jr., quoted in *ibid.*, p.139.
115. Hollis Chenery, quoted in *ibid.*, p.140. Emphasis mine.
116. Simon Hanson, 'The Alliance for Progress, the Fourth Year', *Inter-American Economic Affairs,* **20** (1966) p.62.
117. *ibid.*, p.64.
118. Hanson, *op. cit.*, p.64.

119. Henry Bittermann, *op. cit.*, p.190. For other aspects of the Philippine rescheduling package see Cheryl Payer, *The Debt Trap*, Chapter 3.
120. World Bank, *Annual Report 1970*, pp.47–8.

Chapter 12

121. Peter Körner, Gero Maass, Thomas Siebold and Rainer Teztlaff, *The IMF and the Debt Crisis* (London: Zed Books, 1986) Appendix 1. The cases of Brazil, Cambodia, Chile, Ghana, India and Indonesia are discussed in Payer, *The Debt Trap, passim.*
122. Alexis Rieffel, *The Role of the Paris Club in Managing Debt Problems*, Essays in International Finance No. 161 (Princeton: International Finance Section, Department of Economics, Princeton University, 1985) p.5.
123. Rieffel, p.15.
124. Rieffel, p.13.
125. For example, in Cheryl Payer, *The Debt Trap: The IMF and the Third World* (London: Penguin, 1974 and New York: Monthly Review, 1975) and many other subsequent works.
126. Rieffel, p.8.
127. This is my paraphrase of Rieffel's remarks on Cuba's performance after a 1983 rescheduling in which IMF conditionality could not be imposed because Cuba is not a member of the Fund.

Chapter 13

128. Charles Frank, *op. cit.*, p.31.
129. Bitterman, p.3.
130. *Business Latin America*, 21 March, 1968, p.90.
131. Nelson Rockefeller, *Report on the Americas* (Chicago: Quadrangle Books, 1969) p.87.
132. Task Force on International Development [Peterson commission], *U.S. Foreign Assistance in the 1970s: a new approach*, Report to the President (Washington: Government Printing Office, 1970) p.10.
133. *ibid* p.28.
134. Rosario Green, *El Endeudamiento público externo de México, op. cit.*, p.189.
135. Robert S. McNamara, Speech to United Nations Conference on Trade and Development, 14 April 1972.
136. Lester B. Pearson, *The Crisis of Development* (New York: Praeger for the Council of Foreign Relations, 1969) p.91.

Chapter 14

137. *Business Latin America*, 30 January 1974, pp.35–6, 37–9; 6 February 1974, p.41; 11 December 1974, p.400.
138. R. C. Williams, *et al.*, *International Capital Markets 1981*, IMF Occasional Paper No.7 (Washington: International Monetary Fund, 1981) p.64.
139. Martin Mayer, *The Money Bazaars: Understanding the Banking Revolution Around Us* (New York: E. P. Dutton, 1984) p.239. Emphasis in original.
140. OECD, *Twenty-Five Years of Development Cooperation* (Paris 1985) p.166.
141. Rosario Green, *El endeudamiento público externo de México, op. cit.*, pp.176–7.

142. Jeffrey A. Frieden, 'The Brazilian Borrowing Experience: From Miracle to Débâcle and Back', *Latin American Research Review* **22** (1987) p.99.
143. S. C. Gwynne, *Selling Money* (New York: Penguin 1987) p.105.

Chapter 15

144. Edward S. Mason and Robert E. Asher, *The World Bank since Bretton Woods* (Washington, D.C.: The Brookings Institution, 1973) pp.759–60.
145. *ibid.*, p.180.
146. *Wall Street Journal*, 7 April 1969.
147. Memorandum to Thomas Mann and David Bell from ARA/LA/ECP–Mr. Donald Palmer on Bank Lending Targets, 3 March 1965. In *Microfilm Collection of Declassified Documents* (University Publications of America, 1985) Doc.002832.
148. *Wall Street Journal*, 1 June 1965, p.15.
149. *Wall Street Journal*, 16 March 1967, p.4, and 6 August 1969, p.5.
150. *Wall Street Journal*, 23 July 1971, p.23, and 12 November 1971, p.18.
151 *Wall Street Journal*, 17 November 1971, p.4.
152. World Bank, *Annual Report 1963*–4, p.8.
153. World Bank, *Annual Report 1964*–5, p.57.
154. World Bank, *Annual Report 1965*–6, p.45.
155. World Bank, *Annual Report 1964*–5, p.62. My emphasis.
156. World Bank, *Annual Report 1965*–6, p.45.
157. *ibid.*, p.35.
158. World Bank, *Annual Report 1966–7*, pp.32–3. My emphasis.
159. World Bank, *Annual Report 1971*, p.49.
160. *ibid.*, pp.49–50.
161. *ibid.*, p.52.

Chapter 16

162. Cheryl Payer, *The World Bank: A Critical Analysis* (Monthly Review Press, 1982) pp.128–41.
163. G. A. Costanzo, 'Latin American Myths and Realities', *Barron's*, 31 May 1965.
164. *Business Latin America*, 17 October 1968, pp.335–6.
165. *Business Latin America*, 12 March 1970, p.81.
166. *Wall Street Journal*, 29 April 1971.
167. 'Eager Lenders', *Wall Street Journal* 24 November 1972.
168. 'Uneasy Money', *Wall Street Journal*, 21 May 1973.
169. *Banking*, November 1969, p.45.
170. *Banking*, January 1970, p.52.
171. *Banking*, August 1970, p.42.
172. 'Why the major players allowed it to happen', *International Currency Review* (May 1984) p.21.
173. Theodore Moran, *Multinational Corporations and the Politics of Dependence* (Princeton University Press, 1974); John Deverell and the Latin American Working Group, *Falconbridge: Portrait of a Canadian Mining Multinational* (Toronto: James Lorimer & Company, 1975) p.63.
174. 'Why the Major Players Allowed it to Happen', *op. cit.*, p.24.
175. Christine A. Bogdanowicz-Bindert and Paul M. Sacks, 'The Role of Information: Closing the Barn Door?' in *Uncertain Future: Commercial Banks and*

the Third World, ed. Richard E. Feinberg and Valeriana Kallab (New Brunswick, N.J.: Transaction Books for the Overseas Development Council, 1984) p.72. Chapter 3, 'The Paradise of Little Fat Men', in S. C. Gwynne, *Selling Money: A young banker's account of the great international lending boom–and bust* (New York: Penguin, 1986) is essential reading on this topic.

176. Donella Meadows, *et al.*, *The Limits to Growth* (New York: University Books, 1974).

177. Azizale F. Mohammed and Fabrizio Saccomanni, 'Short-term Banking and Euro-Currency Credits to Developing Countries', *International Monetary Fund Staff Papers*, **20** (1973) p.625.

178. Bahram Nowzad and Richard C. Williams, *External Indebtedness of Developing Countries*, IMF Occasional paper No.3, May 1981, p.31.

179. The US Congress ended this practice in 1983 as part of the law approving a capital increase for the IMF. When it was decreed that rescheduling fees had to be amortised over the life of the rescheduled loans, they instantly became much less attractive to the banks.

180. Pierre Latour in *Euromoney* (October 1975) p.4.

181. David I. Levine, 'Developing Countries and the $150 Billion Euromarket Financing Problem', *Euromoney* (December 1975) p.14.

182. Charles G. Grave, 'U.S. Banks' International Loans Under Scrutiny', *Euromoney* (March 1976) p.13.

Chapter 17

183. Organisation for Economic Cooperation and Development, *Debt Problems of Developing Countries* (Paris: OECD 1974) p.29, para. 93.

184. International Monetary Fund, *Annual Report 1975*, p.3. My emphasis.

185. *ibid.*, p.4.

186. William B. Dale, 'Financing and Adjustment of Payments Imbalances', in John Williamson, ed., *IMF Conditionality* (Washington: Institute for International Economics, 1983) p.7.

187. Council on Foreign Relations, *American Foreign Relations 1975* (New York: New York University Press) p.427–8.

188. *loc. cit.*

189. Harold Lever and Christopher Huhne, *Debt and Danger: The World Financial Crisis* (Harmondsworth: Penguin, 1985) p.55. My emphasis.

190. David Gisselquist, *The Political Economics of International Bank Lending* (New York: Praeger, 1981) p.156. See also by the same author *Oil Prices and Trade Deficits: U.S. Conflicts with Japan and West Germany* (New York: Praeger, 1979).

Chapter 18

191. Until the early 1980s, when exceptions were made for Poland, Mozambique and Cuba. Rieffel, pp.9–10.

192. Alex Rieffel, 'The Role of the Paris Club in Managing Debt Problems', *supra*, p.5.

193. Richard Bernal, 'Transnational Banks, the International Monetary Fund, and external debt of developing countries', *Social and Economic Studies*, **31** (1982) pp.85–6.

194. *IMF Survey*, 7 March 1973, quoted in Bernal, p.82.

195. Jim Browning, 'Inside Story: The Philippines and the IMF', *Asian Wall Street Journal*, 15 August 1979.

196. Cary Reich, 'Why the IMF Shuns a "Super" Role', *Institutional Investor*, September 1977, p.185.

197. This is condensed from Cheryl Payer, 'Tanzania and the World Bank', *Third World Quarterly,* **5** (1983) pp.797–8 and *passim*.

198. As in the case of Tanzania, some of my information on Jamaica comes from a visit to the country and from confidential personal interviews. The interpretations of Jamaica's IMF experience are as varied as the stories in Rashomon; one that conforms to this version is by Manley advisers Norman Girvan, Richard Bernal and Wesley Hughes, 'The IMF and the Third World: The Case of Jamaica', *Development Dialogue,* **2** (1980) pp.123–32.

199. World Bank, *Economic Situation and Prospects of India*, Report No. 3872-IN, 7 April 1982, para. 3.51.

200. *New York Times*, 9 September 1981.

201. International Monetary Fund, *India, Use of Fund Resources–Extended Fund Facility*, EBS/81/198, 4 October 1981. The paragraphs on India contain a drastic condensation of the argument in Cheryl Payer, 'The IMF and India', in Kjell Havnevik, ed., *The IMF and the World Bank in Africa* (Uppsala: Scandinavian Institute for African Studies, 1987) in which this IMF document is quoted.

202. World Bank, *Economic Situation and Prospects of India*, Report No. 3872-IN, 7 April 1982) para. 3.47.

203. Mick Moore, 'On the Political Economy of Stabilization', *World Development* **13**, (1985) p.1,089.

204. Cheryl Payer, *The World Bank: A Critical Analysis* (New York: Monthly Review Press, 1982) p.81.

205. Robin Broad, *Unequal Alliance: The World Bank and the Philippines* (Berkeley: University of California Press, 1988) p.205 and note 1, pp.321–2. My emphasis.

206. Cheryl Payer, 'The Asian Debtors', *Third World Affairs 1988* (London: Third World Foundation) p.296.

207. Cheryl Payer: 'The IMF in the 1980s: What has it learned; What have we learned about it?' *Third World Affairs 1985* (London: Third World Foundation, 1985) p.8.

208. This crisis was examined in Cheryl Payer, *The Debt Trap*, Chapter 3. The following discussion draws heavily on Philip Wellons, *Borrowing by Developing Countries on the Eurocurrency Markets*, Paris: Development Centre of the OECD, 1977, Chapter 6.

Chapter 19

209. Except in the case of Iran, the classic exception which proves the rule. Iran had the means to pay and wanted to pay its debt service; it was unable to pay because, as a result of the hostage crisis, President Carter had frozen the funds held in US banks from which payment was to be made.

210. Martin Mayer, *The Money Bazaars, op. cit.*, pp.246–7.

211. *Business Week*, 3 October 1983, p.132.

212. Personal communication, 13 January 1990.

213. James S. Henry, 'Where the Money Went', *The New Republic*, 14 April 1986, pp.22, 23.

214. Henry, p.22.

215. Bogdanowicz-Bindert and Sacks, *op. cit.*, p.71.

216. *loc. cit.* My emphasis.

217. Robert Devlin and Michael Mortimore, *Los Bancos Transnacionales, el Estado y el Endeudamiento Externo en Bolivia*, Estudios e Informes de la Cepal No. 26 (Santiago de Chile 1983) pp.92, 99.

218. *Global Financial Intermediation and Policy Analysis* (Citibank, 1980), quoted in 'Why the Major Players Allowed it to Happen', *International Currency Review*, May 1984, p.22. Emphasis mine. The conclusion, by the way, is entirely tautological, since net present value is a function of the rate of interest. If front-end fees are collected in addition, they are icing on the cake.

219. 'Final Report of the Task Force on Non-Concessional Flows to the Joint Ministerial Committee of the Boards of Governors of the Bank and the Fund on the Transfer of Resources to the Developing Countries', (5 April 1982) quoted in 'Why the Major Players Allowed it to Happen', *ibid.*, p.25.

Chapter 20

220. Peter Field, David Shirreff and William Ollard, 'The IMF and Central Banks Flex Their Muscles', *Euromoney*, January 1983, p.41.

221. E.g. William R. Cline, *International Debt and the Stability of the World Economy* (Washington: Institute for International Economics, 1983) which received wide coverage in the media.

Chapter 21

222. See Cheryl Payer, *The Debt Trap: the IMF and the Third World* (New York: Monthly Review Press, 1974) for an early critique. See also the bibliography listed in footnote 1 of Cheryl Payer, 'The IMF in the 1980s: What has it learned, What have we learned about it?' *Third World Affairs 1985* (London: Third World Foundation) p.1.

223. *New York Times*, 3 October 1985.

224. For a discussion of World Bank project lending, see Cheryl Payer, *The World Bank: A Critical Analysis* (New York: Monthly Review Press, 1982).

225. World Bank, *Annual Report 1980*, p.67.

226. *ibid.*, p.57.

227. World Bank, *Annual Report 1982*, p.35; Edmar L. Bacha and Richard E. Feinberg, 'The World Bank and Structural Adjustment in Latin America', *World Development* **14** (1986) p.338.

228. Robin Broad, *Unequal Alliance: The World Bank, The International Monetary Fund, and the Philippines* (Berkeley: University of California Press, 1988) pp.98–102. This is at present the best available case study of a World Bank SAL in a particular country.

229. *New York Times*, 26 April 1980.

230. Pierre M. Landell-Mills, 'Structural Adjustment Lending: Early Experience' *Finance and Development*, 1981, pp.17–21. Other works on structural adjustment by World Bank staff members include Bela Balassa, *Structural Adjustment Policies in Developing Countries*, World Bank Staff Working Paper No. 464, (July 1981); Ernest Stern, 'World Bank Financing of Structural Adjustment', in John Williamson, ed., *IMF Conditionality* (Washington, D.C.: Institute for International Economics, 1983); P. Hasan, *Growth and Structural Adjustment in East Asia*, World Bank Staff Working Paper No. 529; Stanley Please, *The Hobbled Giant: Essays on the World Bank* (Boulder, Co.: Westview Press, 1984); Please, 'The World Bank: Lending for Structural Adjustment', in Richard Feinberg and Valeriana Kallab, eds.,

Adjustment Crisis in the Third World (New Brunswick, N.J.: Transaction Books for the Overseas Development Council, 1984).

231. 'In cases with a history of detailed import licensing, major liberalization is inconsistent with reducing import levels because the true price elasticity is very low. Market incentives . . . seem to result . . . shifting the balance of imports away from maintenance and production inputs toward consumer amenities. This is not necessarily an allocational improvement, as it is likely to maximize the cost of any import reduction and, indeed, to erode the future export base.' Reginald Green, 'IMF Stabilisation and Structural Adjustment in sub-Saharan Africa: are they technically compatible?' *IDS Bulletin,* **16** (1985) p.64.

232. '[T]here was little to suggest that conditionality has enhanced the role of supply-side approaches which might increase food output without necessarily increasing prices . . . The record of [African] countries over the recent past leaves few grounds for optimism that the food-insecure will be protected during difficult times of austerity and adjustment.' Lionel Demery and Tony Addison, 'Food Insecurity and Adjustment Policies in sub-Saharan Africa: A Review of the Evidence', *Development Policy Review*, **5** (1987) pp.191, 194.

233. Broad, *op. cit.*, Chapter 7; James Cypher, 'Strings Attached: World Bank tightens control of Third World economies', *Dollars and Sense,* **152** (1989) p.11.

234. [In Africa] 'Privatization equals foreign management'. *New York Times*, 30 July 1987.

235. Broad, *op. cit.*, pp.148–55.

236. 'To be only mildly whimsical, the Bank should at least complement its precondition that a SAP candidate negotiate a [drawing at nine per cent interest] with the Fund with the precondition for a low or lower middle income candidate that it must *not* draw on it.' Green, *op. cit.,* pp.67–8.

237. Alejandro Foxley, *Latin American Experiments in Neoconservative Economics* (Berkeley: University of California Press, 1983) p.41.

Chapter 22

238. Henry Breck, 'The Maltese Falcon of Foreign Debt', *Wall Street Journal*, 5 February 1987.

239. Peter Truell, 'Foreign Loans Buoyed by U.S. Debt Strategy', *Wall Street Journal*, 19 July 1989.

240. Peter Truell, 'Bank Lending Now Linchpin of Debt Plan', *Wall Street Journal*, 28 July 1989.

Chapter 23

241. Henry R. Breck (as his *alter ego* Quickfix Kelly), 'African Relief, Spelled D-E-F-A-U-L-T', *Wall Street Journal*, 7 November 1986.

242. Anne Krueger, 'Aid in the Development Process', *Research Observer* **1** (1986) p. 65. Krueger, a World Bank economist, draws from this analysis of private capital market failure 'a strong analytical case for official assistance on commercial terms'. That World Bank intellectuals find new justifications for more public lending is not surprising, but I cannot perceive how more borrowing *on commercial terms* will solve the problem. Clearly it would simply prolong the agony.

243. The Bolivian plan is explained in World Bank, *World Debt Tables 1987–88*, Box 4, p. xvii.

244. Carlos F. Diaz Alejandro, 'Stories of the 1930s for the 1980s', in Aspe Armella, Rudiger Dornbusch and Maurice Obstfield, eds., *Financial Policies and the*

World Capital Markets (Chicago: University of Chicago Press, 1980) pp. 25–31; Henry C. Wallich, 'The Future of Latin American Dollar Bonds', *American Economic Review*, **33** (1943) pp. 321–2.

245. Anatole Kaletsky, *The Costs of Default* (New York: Priority Press, 1985) pp. 4–5.

246. US Senator Bill Bradley, with urgency in his voice, interviewed on 'Morning Edition', National Public Radio, 6 October 1987.

247. This important and heartbreaking story is told in Jackie Roddick (ed.), *The Dance of the Millions: Latin America and the Debt Crisis* (London: Latin American Bureau, 1988) Chapter 9.

248. *Wall Street Journal*, 14 August 1987.

249. Laurence W. Levine [President, Argentine–American Chamber of Commerce], letter to the *Wall Street Journal*, 22 January 1988.

250. See, among others, S. Karene Witcher, 'Should Debtors Repudiate? Some feel it would hurt less than current austerity', *Wall Street Journal*, 22 June 1984.

251. Gary Hector, 'Third World Debt: The Bomb is Defused', *Fortune*, 18 February 1985, p. 42.

252. For a thorough and fascinating analysis, see Anatole Kaletsky, *The Cost of Default* (New York: Priority Press for the Twentieth Century Fund, 1985).

253. Luiz Carlos Bresser Pereira, in a private communication to the author, 31 July 1989.

254. Luiz Bresser Pereira, 'Da crise fiscal à redução da dívida', in Bresser Pereira, ed., *Dívida Externa: Crise e Soluções* (São Paulo: Editora Brasiliense, 1989) pp. 48–50.

255. Anthony Marcus and Jeffrey Franks, Letter to the editor, *New York Times*, 6 January 1990.

256. Reported by Kai Bird and Max Holland in *The Nation*, 26 February 1983.

257. *International Herald Tribune*, 31 December 1979.

258. Barbara Stallings, *Banker to the Third World: US Portfolio Investment in Latin America, 1900–1986* (Berkeley: University of California Press, 1987) pp. 77–80.

259. Benjamin Weiner, 'When We Forgave (or Forgot) Our Debtors', *Wall Street Journal*, 6 November 1983.

260. Edward S. Mason and Robert E. Asher, *The World Bank Since Bretton Woods* (Washington, DC: Brookings Institution, 1973). pp. 155–8.

261. Within the United States also, lenders have very short memories, as this item from the 13 September 1989, *Wall Street Journal* shows:

> Washington Public Power Supply System, famous for the biggest default in municipal bond industry, returned to the market yesterday with a huge new tax-exempt issue.
>
> But despite its past sins, WPPSS, a nuclear-power agency irreverently known as 'Whoops,' received what its investment bankers called a warm welcome . . .
>
> Some specialists said yesterday's offering represents a classic example of how short a memory many bond underwriters and professional investors have . . . [T]he past no longer seems relevant to many investors.

'Whoops' defaulted on $2.25 billion worth of bonds in 1983, only six years earlier.

Chapter 24

262. Neil H. Jacoby, *US Aid to Taiwan: A Study of Foreign Aid, Self-Help, and Development* (New York: Praeger, 1966) p. 243 and *passim*.

263. Cheryl Payer, 'The Asian Debtors', *Third World Affairs 1988* (London: Third World Foundation) p. 298, and Morgan Guaranty Trust Company, *World Financial Markets*, January 1987, Table 1.

264. Robert S. Ozaki, *The Control of Imports and Foreign Capital in Japan* (New York: Praeger, 1972) p. xv. In another work Ozaki even denies the idea that Japan's growth could be described as 'export-led'; exports represent between 10 and 13 per cent of GNP, a smaller share than in many European states. Ozaki, 'The Political Economy of Japan's Foreign Relations', in Ozaki, ed., *Japan's Foreign Relations: A Global Search for Economic Security* (Boulder: Westview Press, 1985) p. 6.

265. The phrase is from Thorkil Casse, *The Non-Conventional Approach to Stability: The Case of South Korea* (Copenhagen: Centre for Development Research, 1985) p. 9.

266. Casse, p.6. This source emphasises the fact that South Korea benefited from a huge ($4 billion) low-interest loan from Japan in 1982, effectively a bail-out on more generous terms than was made available to Latin American debtors. On the loan, see also Susan Strange, 'Protectionism and World Politics', *International Organization*, **39** (1985) pp. 250–51.

267. This of course does not mean that protecting markets alone will guarantee export success. The model contains many complex features, some of which are compatible with IMF/World Bank ideology, others, such as the heavy government control of and generous government subsidies to industry, which are not.

268. Casse, p. 91.

269. In addition to the Casse work, see Eddy Lee, 'Export-Led Industrialisation in Asia: An Overview' in Eddy Lee, ed., *Export-Led Industrialisation and Development* (Asian Employment Programme, 1981); Colin I. Bradford, Jr., 'Increasing IMF/World Bank Cooperation', Testimony before US House of Representatives Committee on Banking, Finance, and Urban Affairs, Subcommittee on International Development Institutions and Finance and Subcommittee on International Finance, Trade, and Monetary Policy, 25 July 1985, and Cheryl Payer, 'The Asian Debtors', *Third World Affairs 1988* (London: Third World Foundation) for similar criticism of the East Asian model.

Chapter 25

270. Sheik Mohammed Abdou, a 'highly respected' Egyptian Pan-Islamist, is reported to have made this remark in 1884 to the British who were then occupying Egypt, according to the *Wall Street Journal* of 3 September 1987. For an account of how foreign capital wrought economic and political havoc in nineteenth-century Egypt, see John Marlowe, *Spoiling the Egyptians* (New York: St. Martin's Press, 1975).

271. Adrian Lajous, 'A Note to Mexico's Creditors: No More Loans Please', *Wall Street Journal*, 2 October 1987. Lajous confessed to being a reformed 'foreign-money junky'; he was an executive director of the World Bank 1970–72 and former head of Banco Nacional de Commercio Exterior 1979–82.

272. An Indian official quoted in Teresa Hayter, *Aid: Rhetoric and Reality* (London: Pluto Press, 1985) p. 93.

273. John Kenneth Galbraith, *The Nature of Mass Poverty* (Cambridge, 1979) pp. v–vi.

274. Joan Robinson, *Contributions to Modern Economics* (New York: Academic Press, 1978) pp. 220–1.

275. 'A Global Overcapacity Hurts Many Industries; No Easy Cure is Seen', *Wall Street Journal*, 9 March 1987; Louis Uchitelle, 'A Worldwide Glut Crisis', *New York Times*, 17 December 1986. Foreign debt is listed as one of the causes of the overcapacity crisis in the *Wall Street Journal* article.

276. See the discussion of the Sicartsa project in Mexico, *infra*, p. 120.

277. Frank Church, 'Farewell to Foreign Aid: A Liberal Takes Leave', *Congressional Record*, 29 October 1971, p. 38256.

278. The author worked as an intern in the US Agency of International Development in the summer of 1965. At that time every project funded by AID had to be 'cleared' by the Departments of Commerce or Agriculture which checked to make sure they would not compete with American business.

279. John Kenneth Galbraith, 'A Positive Approach to Aid', *Foreign Affairs*, **39**, (1961) p. 449.

280. I have benefited from discussions on this point with Peter Thompson of the Canadian International Development Agency and from reading his unpublished doctoral thesis based on his experiences in Bangladesh. For a popularly written book making some similar points, see Eugene Linden, *The Alms Race: The Impact of American Voluntary Aid Abroad* (New York: Random House, 1976).

281. Victor Mallet, 'Where the aid money goes', *Financial Times*, 30 September 1988.

282. Estimates for the period 1977–87 appear in 'LDC Debt Reduction: A Critical Appraisal', *World Financial Markets* (Morgan Guaranty Trust Company) 1988 Issue 8, 30 December 1988, Tables 7 and 8, p. 9.

283. Rita Tullberg, 'Military-related debt in non-oil developing countries', SIPRI Yearbook 1985, quoted in *Bulletin of Peace Proposals*, **17** (1986) p. 261. See also Thomas Straubhaar, 'The Economics of Third World Arms Imports', *Intereconomics* May/June 1986, pp. 137–41; Michael Brzoska, 'The Accumulation of Military Debt', *IDOC Internazionale* 2/87, pp. 13–16; Nicole Ball, 'Security Expenditure and Economic Growth in Developing Countries', in *Pugwash Annals 1985* (London: Macmillan, 1986); John J. Fialka, 'Easy U.S. Credit Helps Sell Arms; Repayment Can Be Another Matter', *Wall Street Journal*, 13 June 1984; Doug Bandow, 'Aid Money That Just Buys Guns', *Wall Street Journal*, 14 June 1988.

284. Jeffrey A. Frieden, 'The Brazilian Borrowing Experience: From Miracle to Debâcle and Back', *Latin American Research Review* **XXII** (1989) p.96.

285. Anatole Kaletsky, *The Costs of Default* (New York: Priority Press, 1985) p. 5.

286. Robin Broad, *Unequal Alliance: The World Bank, the International Monetary Fund, and the Philippines* (Berkeley: University of California Press, 1988) p.197.

287. Philip Wellons, 'Banks and the Export Credit Wars: Mixed Credits in the Sicartsa Financing', in Rita M. Rodriguez, ed., *The Export–Import Bank at Fifty* (Lexington Books, 1987) pp. 196, 198.

288. Philip Wellons, ibid., p. 196.

289. Keith Griffin, *International Inequality and National Poverty* (London: Macmillan, 1978) p. 62. Emphasis mine.

290. Griffin, 'Foreign capital', p. 79. I have paraphrased his algebraic formulation to make it accessible to non-economists.

291. Charles P. Kindleberger, 'Debt Situation of the Developing Countries in Historical Perspective', in Stephen H. Goodman, ed., *Financing and Risk in*

Developing Countries (New York: Praeger, 1978) p. 9. My emphasis.

292. Griffin, 'Foreign capital', p. 68.

293. John Knapp, 'Capital Exports and Growth', *Economic Journal* **67** (1957) p. 444.

294. Albert Fishlow, 'The State of Latin American Economies', in Inter-American Development Bank, *Economic and Social Progress in Latin America: External Debt: Crisis and Adjustment* (Washington: Inter-American Development Bank, 1988) p. 135.

295. Keith Griffin, in a letter to the author, 18 July 1989.

296. Since a large number of Third World countries are being forced by the IMF and World Bank to expand their exports in the small number of commodities which they produce, their competition among themselves drives the price to rockbottom levels.

297. That would mean exchange and import controls, an IMF no-no.

Chapter 26

298. André Gunder Frank has long advocated this point of view. See his 'The Development of Underdevelopment', in Charles K. Wilber, ed., *The Political Economy of Development and Underdevelopment*, 2nd edition (New York: Random House, 1979) pp. 77–90. A recent book of monographs supporting this interpretation is Ian Brown, ed., *The Economies of Africa and Asia in the Inter-war Depression* (London: Routledge, 1989).

299. US bankruptcy law is more generous than that of other countries.

Bibliography

BOOKS AND ARTICLES

Anonymous (1984), "Why the Major Players Allowed It To Happen," *International Currency Review* (May).

Avramović, Dragoslav and Ravi Gulhati (1960), *Debt Servicing Problems of Low-Income Countries 1956–58*, Baltimore: Johns Hopkins Press for the IBRD.

Avramović, Dragoslav, et al (1964), *Economic Growth and External Debt*, Baltimore: Johns Hopkins Press for the IBRD.

Bacha, Edmar L. and Richard E. Feinberg (1986), "The World Bank and Structural Adjustment in Latin America," *World Development* 14, No.3.

Balassa, Bela (1971) *Development Strategies in Some Developing Countries: A Comparative Study.* Baltimore: Johns Hopkins University for the World Bank.

——— (1981), *Structural Adjustment Policies in Developing Countries,* World Bank Working Paper No.464, July.

Ball, Nicole (1986), "Security Expenditure and Economic Growth in Developing Countries," *Pugwash Annals 1985*. London: Macmillan.

Bandow, Doug (1988), "Aid Money That Just Buys Guns," *Wall Street Journal*, June 14.

Bernal, Richard (1982), "Transnational Banks, the International Monetary Fund, and External Debt of Developing Countries," *Social and Economic Studies* 13, 4.

Berrill, K.E. (1963), "Foreign Capital and Take-Off," in W.W. Rostow, ed., *The Economics of Take-Off into Sustained Growth*, New York, St. Martin's Press.

Bhagwati, Jagdish (1978), *Anatomy and Consequences of Exchange Control Regimes.* Cambridge: Ballinger for the National Bureau of Economic Research.

Bittermann, Henry (1973), *The Refunding of International Debt*, Durham, N.C., Duke University Press.

Bogdanowicz-Bindert, Christine A. and Paul M. Sacks (1984), "The Role of Information: Closing the Barn Door?" in Richard E. Feinberg and Valeriana Kallab, eds., *Uncertain Future: Commercial Banks and the Third World.* New Brunswick, N.J.: Transaction Books for the Overseas Development Council.

Bortis, Heinrich (1979), *Foreign Resources and Economic Development from the Early Fifties to the Oil Crisis*, Institut des Sciences Economiques et Sociales de l'Université de Fribourg, Documents économiques No.11, Fribourg, Editions Universitaires.

Bradford, Jr., Colin I., (1985), "Increasing IMF/World Bank Cooperation," Testimony before U.S. House of Representatives Committee on Banking, Finance and Urban Affairs, Subcommittee on International Development

Institutions and Finance and Subcommittee on International Finance, Trade and Monetary Policy, June 25.
Breck, Henry R. (1986) "African Relief, Spelled D-E-F-A-U-L-T," *Wall Street Journal*, November 7.
—— (1987), "The Maltese Falcon of Foreign Debt," *Wall Street Journal*, February 5.
Bresser Pereira, Luiz (1989), "Da crise fiscal a reducao da divida," in *Dívida Externa: Crise e Soluções*, ed. Luiz Bresser Pereira. São Paulo: Editora Brasiliense.
Broad, Robin (1988), *Unequal Alliance: The World Bank, the International Monetary Fund and the Philippines*. Berkeley, University of California Press.
Brown, E. Phelps (1972), "The Underdevelopment of Economics," *Economic Journal* 82, (March).
Brown, Ian, ed. (1989), *The Economic of Africa and Asia in the Inter-War Depression*. London: Routledge.
Browning, Jim (1979), "Inside Story: The Philippines and the IMF," *Asian Wall Street Journal* (August 15).
Brzoska, Michael (1987) "The Accumulation of Military Debt," *IDOC Internazionale* 2/87.
Bullock, Charles J., John H. Williams, and Rufus S. Tucker (1919), "The Balance of Trade of the United States," in *The Review of Economic Statistics* 1.
Casse, Thorkil (1985), *The Non-Conventional Approach to Stability: The Case of South Korea*. Copenhagen: Centre for Development Research.
Chenery, H.B. (1964), "Objectives and Criteria of Foreign Assistance," in G. Ranis, ed., *The United States and the Developing Economies*. New York: W.W. Norton.
—— and Alan Strout (1966), "Foreign Assistance and Economic Development," *American Economic Review* 56, 4.
Church, Frank (1971), "Farewell to Foreign Aid: A Liberal Takes Leave," *Congressional Record*, October 29.
Clark, Colin (1950), "The World Will Save Money in the 1950s," *Fortune*, (July).
Cline, William R. (1983), *International Debt and the Stability of the World Economy*. Washington, Institute for International Economics.
Costanzo, G.A. (1965), "Latin American Myths and Realities," Barron's (May 31).
Council on Foreign Relations (1975), *American Foreign Relations 1975*. New York, New York University Press.
Cypher, James (1989), "Strings Attached: World Bank Tightens Control of Third World economies," *Dollars and Sense*, No.152, December.
Dale, William B. (1983), "Financing and Adjustment of Payments Imbalances," in John Williamson, ed., *IMF Conditionality*. Washington, Institute for International Economics.
Demery, Lionel and Tony Addison (1987), "Food Insecurity and Adjustment Policies in sub-Saharan Africa: A Review of the Evidence," *Development Policy Review*, 5.
Deverell, John and the Latin American Working Group (1975), *Falconbridge: Portrait of a Canadian Mining Multinational*. Toronto, James Lorimer & Company.
Devlin, Robert and Michael Mortimore (1983), "Los Bancos Transnacionales, el Estado y el Endeudamiento Externo in Bolivia", *Estudios e Informes de la Cepal* no.26. Santiago de Chile, CEPAL.
Diaz Alejandro, Carlos (1980), "Stories of the 1930s for the 1980s," in *Financial*

Policies and the World Capital Markets, Aspe Armella, Rudiger Dornbusch, and Maurice Obstfield, eds. Chicago: University of Chicago Press.

Domar, E.D. (1950), "The Effect of Foreign Investment on the Balance of Payments," *American Economic Review* 40 (December).

Edgerton, Russell (1967), "The Creation of the Development Loan Fund," Ph.D. Thesis, Columbia University.

Fialka, John (1984), "Easy U.S. Credit Helps Sell Arms; Repayment Can be Another Matter," *Wall Street Journal*, June 13.

Field, Peter, David Shirreff and William Ollard (1983), "The IMF and Central Banks Flex Their Muscles," *Euromoney*, January.

Fishlow, Albert (1988), "The State of Latin American Economies," in *Economic and Social Progress in Latin America: External Debt: Crisis and Adjustment*, Washington. Inter-American Development Bank.

Foxley, Alejandro (1983), *Latin American Experiments in Neoconservative Economics*. Berkeley, University of California Press.

Frank, André Gunder (1979), "The Development of Underdevelopment," in *The Political Economy of Development and Underdevelopment*, 2nd. edition, ed. Charles K. Wilber. New York: Random House.

Frank, Jr., Charles R. (1972), "Debt and Terms of Aid," in Overseas Development Council, *Assisting Developing Countries*. New York: Praeger.

Frieden, Jeffrey A. (1987), "The Brazilian Borrowing Experience: from Miracle to Debacle and Back," *Latin American Research Review* 22, 1.

——— (1961), "A Positive Approach to Aid," *Foreign Affairs*, 39, no.3 (April).

Galbraith, John Kenneth (1979), *The Nature of Mass Poverty*, Cambridge.

GATT-Fly (1985 and later supplements), *Debt Bondage or Self-Reliance*, Toronto.

George, Susan (1988), *A Fate Worse Than Debt*, New York, Grove Press.

Girvan, Norman, Richard Bernal and Wesley Hughes (1980), "The IMF and the Third World: The Case of Jamaica," *Development Dialogue* 2, 1.

Gisselquist, David (1979), *Oil Prices and Trade Deficits: U.S. Conflicts with Japan and West Germany*. New York, Praeger.

Gisselquist, David (1981), *The Political Economics of International Bank Lending*. New York, Praeger.

Grant, James P. (1989), *The State of the World's Children 1989*, New York, Oxford University Press for UNICEF.

Grave, Charles G. (1976), "U.S. Banks' International Loans Under Scrutiny," *Euromoney* (March).

Gray Report (1950), *Report to the President on Foreign Economic Policies*, Washington.

Green, Reginald (1985), "IMF Stabilisation and Structural Adjustment in sub-Saharan Africa: are they technically compatible?" *IDS Bulletin* 16, no.3.

Green, Rosario (1976), *El endeudamiento publico externo de Mexico, 1940–1973*, Mexico, El Colegio de Mexico.

Griffin, Keith and Jeffrey James (1980), *The Transition to Equalitarian Development*, London, Macmillan.

Griffin, Keith (1969), *Underdevelopment in Spanish America: an Interpretation*, London, Allen & Unwin.

——— (1978), *International Inequality and National Poverty*. London: Macmillan.

——— (1986), "Doubts About Aid", in *IDS Bulletin* 17, 2.

——— and J.L. Enos (1970), "Foreign Assistance: Objectives and Consequences," in *Economic Development and Cultural Change* 18 (April).

Griffith-Jones, Stephany (1982), "Transnational Finance and Latin American National Development," IDS Working Paper No.175 (July).

Gwynne, S.C. (1986), *Selling Money: A Young Banker's Account of the Great International Lending Boom–and Bust*, Harmondsworth, Penguin.

Hansen, Alvin (1960), *Economic Issues of the 1960s*, New York, McGraw-Hill.

Hanson, Simon (1966), "The Alliance for Progress, the Fourth Year," *Inter-American Economic Affairs* 20, 2 (1966).

Hasan, P. (1982), *Growth and Structural Adjustment in East Asia*, World Bank Staff Working Paper No.529.

Hayter, Teresa (1985), *Aid: Rhetoric and Reality*, London: Pluto Press.

Hector, Gary (1985), "Third World Debt: The Bomb is Defused," *Fortune*, February 18.

Henry, James S. (1986), "Where the Money Went," *The New Republic*, April 14.

Hinshaw, Randall (1946), "Foreign Investment and American Employment," Papers and Proceedings of the 58th Annual Meeting of the American Economic Association, *American Economic Review*.

Hirshman, Albert O. (1981), *Essays in Trespassing*, Cambridge University Press.

Høst-Madsen, Poul (1966), "What Does it Mean: a Deficit in the Balance of Payments?" *Finance and Development* 3 (September).

International Monetary Fund (1981), *India, Use of Fund Resources–Extended Fund Facility*, EBS/81/198, October 4, 1981.

Issacson, Walter (1986), *The Wise Men: Six Friends and the World They Made: Acheson, Bohlen, Harriman, Kennan, Lovett, McCloy*, New York, Simon and Schuster.

Jacoby, Neil H. (1966), *U.S. Aid to Taiwan: A Study of Foreign Aid, Self-Help, and Development*. New York, Praeger.

Kaletsky, Anatole (1985), *The Costs of Default*. New York: Priority Press.

Keynes, John Maynard, *Collected Writings*, vol. XXI. London: Macmillan.

Kindleberger, C.P. (1978a), "Debt Situation of the Developing Countries in Historical Perspective," in *Financing and Risk in Developing Countries*, ed. Stephen H. Goodman. New York: Praeger.

——— (1978b), *Manias, Panics, and Crashes: A History of Financial Crises*, New York, Basic Books.

Knapp, John (1957), "Capital Exports and Growth," *Economic Journal* 67, September.

Körner, Peter, Gero Maass, Thomas Siebold and Rainer Tetzlaff (1986), *The IMF and the Debt Crisis*, London, Zed Books.

Koht Norbye, Ole David (1987), "The International Debt Burden in Norway, 1865–1985," unpublished, Bergen, Norway.

Kraeger, Ann (1978), *Foreign Trade Regimes and Economic Development: Liberalization Attempts and Consequences*. New York: National Bureau of Economic Research.

——— (1986), "Aid in the Development Process," *Research Observer* 1, no.1.

Lajous, Adrian (1987), "A Note to Mexico's Creditors: No More Loans Please," *Wall Street Journal*, October 2.

Landell-Mills, Pierre M. (1981), "Structural Adjustment Lending: Early Experience," *Finance and Development*, December.

Lary, Hal B. (1946), "The Domestic Effects of Foreign Investment," Papers and Proceedings of the 58th Annual Meeting of the American Economic Association, *American Economic Review*.

Lee, Eddy (1981), "Export-Led Industrialisation in Asia: An Overview," in *Export-led Industrialization and Development*, ed. Eddy Lee. Bangkok: Asian Employment Programme.

Leontief, Wassily (1971), "Theoretical Assumptions and Nonobserved Facts," *American Economic Review* 56, 1 (March).

Lever, Harold and Christopher Huhne (1985), *Debt and Danger: The World Financial Crisis*, Harmondsworth, Penguin.

Levine, David I. (1975), "Developing Countries and the $150 Billion Euromarket Financing Problem," *Euromoney* (December).

Levinson, Jerome, and Juan de Onis (1970), *The Alliance That Lost its Way: A Critical Report on the Alliance for Progress*, Chicago, Quadrangle Books.

Linden, Eugene (1976), *The Alms Race: The Impact of American Voluntary Aid Abroad*, New York, Random House.

Little, I.M., Tibor Scitavsky, and Maurice Scott (1970), *Industry and Trade in Some Developing Countries: A Comparative Study*. London and New York: Oxford University Press for the OECD Development Centre.

Little, Jane Suedon (1975), *Eurodollars: The Money-Market Gypsies*, New York, Harper & Row.

Magdoff, Harry (1969), *The Age of Imperialism*, New York, Monthly Review Press.

Mallett, Victor (1988), "Where the Aid Money Goes," *Financial Times*, September 30.

Marlowe, John (1975), *Spoiling the Egyptians*. New York, St. Martins Press.

Mason, Edward S. and Robert E. Asher (1973), *The World Bank Since Bretton Woods*. Washington, The Brookings Institution.

Mayer, Martin (1984), *The Money Bazaars: Understanding the Banking Revolution Around Us*. New York, E.P. Dutton.

McNamara, Robert S. (1972), Speech to United Nations Conference on Trade and Development, April 14.

Meadows, Donella et al (1974), *The Limits to Growth*. New York, University Books.

Mikesell, Raymond (1983), *The Economics of Foreign Aid and Self-sustaining Development*, Boulder, Co., Westview.

Millikan, Max, and Walt Whitman Rostow (1957), *A Proposal: Keys to an Effective Foreign Policy*, New York, Harper.

Millikan, Max, and Donald Blackmer, eds. (1961), *The Emerging Nations: Their Growth and United States Policy*. Boston: Little Brown & Company.

Mohammed, Azizale F. and Fabrizio Saccomanni (1973), "Short-term Banking and Eurocurrency Credits to Developing Countries," *International Monetary Fund Staff Papers* 20.

Moore, Mick (1985), "On the Political Economy of Stabilization," *World Development* 13, 9.

Moran, Theodore (1974), *Multinational Corporations and the Politics of Dependence*, Princeton, Princeton University Press.

National Planning Association (1944), *New Opportunities in World Trade*.

North, Douglass C. (1962), "International Capital Movements in Historical Perspective," in Raymond Mikesell, ed., *U.S. Private and Government Investment Abroad*, Eugene, Oregon, University of Oregon Press.

Nowzad, Bahram and Richard C. Williams (1981), *External Indebtedness of Developing Countries*, IMF Occasional Paper no.3. (May).

OECD (1974), *Debt Problems of Developing Countries*, Paris.

——— (1985), *Twenty-five Years of Development Cooperation*, Paris.

Overseas Development Council (1974), *New Directions in Development*, New York: Praeger.
Ozaki, Robert S. (1972), *The Control of Imports and Foreign Capital in Japan*. New York: Praeger.
——— (1985), "The Political Economy of Japan's Foreign Relations," in Robert S. Ozaki, ed., *Japan's Foreign Relations: A Global Search for Economic Security*. Boulder: Westview Press.
Paul, Randolph E. (1947), *Taxation for Prosperity*, Indianapolis, Ind., Bobbs-Merrill.
Payer, Cheryl (1975), *The Debt Trap: The IMF and the Third World*, Harmondsworth, Penguin.
——— (1982), *The World Bank: A Critical Analysis*, New York, Monthly Review.
——— (1983), "Tanzania and the World Bank," *Third World Quarterly* 5, 4.
——— (1985a), "The IMF in the 1980s: what has it learned, what have we learned about it?" in *Third World Affairs 1985*. London, Third World Foundation.
——— (1985b), "The Politics of Intervention: The Italian Crisis of 1976," in Stephen Resnick and Richard Wolff, *Rethinking Marxism*, Brooklyn, Automedia.
——— (1987), "The IMF and India," in *The IMF and the World Bank in Africa*, ed. Kjell Havnevik, Uppsala, Scandinavian Institute of African Studies.
——— (1988), "The Asian Debtors," *Third World Affairs 1988*. London, Third World Foundation.
Pearson, Lester B. (1969), *The Crisis of Development*, New York, Praeger, for the Council of Foreign Relations.
Platt, D.C.M. (1984), *Foreign Finance in Continental Europe and the United States, 1815–1870*, London, George Allen & Unwin.
Please, Stanley (1984a), *The Hobbled Giant: Essays on the World Bank*. Boulder: Westview Press.
——— (1984b), "The World Bank: Lending for Structural Adjustment," in *Adjustment Crisis in the Third World*, eds. Richard Feinberg and Valeriana Kallab. Washington, Overseas Development Council.
Reich, Cary (1977), "Why the IMF Shuns a 'Super' Role," *Institutional Investor* (September).
Rieffel, Alexis (1985), *The Role of the Paris Club in Managing Debt Problems*, Essays in International Finance No.161, Princeton, International Finance Section, Department of Economics, Princeton University.
Robinson, Joan (1978), *Contributions to Modern Economics*, New York: Academic Press.
Rockefeller, Nelson (1969), *Report on the Americas*, Chicago, Quadrangle Press.
Roddick, Jackie (ed.) (1988), *The Dance of the Millions: Latin America and the Debt Crisis*. London: Latin America Bureau.
Rosenstein-Rodan, Paul (1961), "International Aid for Underdeveloped Countries," *Review of Economics and Statistics*.
Rostow, W.W. (1960), *The Stages of Economic Growth: A Non-Communist Manifesto*, Cambridge University Press.
——— (1985), *Eisenhower, Kennedy, and Foreign Aid*, Austin, Texas, University of Texas Press.
Samuelson, Paul (1976), *Economics*, 10th Ed., New York, McGraw-Hill.
Schmidt, Wilson and Barbara R. Berman (1965), "Default of International Public Debts," *The National Banking Review*. Article by Schmidt in 2:403–5 (March) with comment by Berman in 2:569–71 (June).
Sobhan, Rehman (1982), *The Crisis of External Dependence: The Political Economy*

of Foreign Aid to Bangladesh, London, Zed Press.
Solomon, Robert (1985), "The United States as a Debtor in the 19th Century," Brookings Discussion Papers in International Economics, No.28 (May).
Stallings, Barbara (1987), *Banker to the Third World: U.S. Portfolio Investments in Latin America, 1900–1986*. Berkeley: University of California Press.
Stern, Ernest (1983), "World Bank Financing of Structural Adjustment," in *IMF Conditionality*, John Williamson, ed. Washington: Institute of International Economics.
Strange, Susan (1985), "Protectionism and World Politics," *International Organization* 39, no.2, Spring.
Straubhaar, Thomas (1986), "The Economics of Third World Arms Imports," *Intereconomics* May/June.
Task Force on International Development [Peterson Commission] (1970), *U.S. Foreign Assistance in the 1970s: a new approach:* report to the President. Washington, Government Printing Office.
Truell, Peter (1989a), "Foreign Loans Buoyed by U.S. Debt Strategy," *Wall Street Journal*, July 19.
——— (1989b), "Bank Lending New Linchpin of Debt Plan," *Wall Street Journal*, July 28.
Tullberg, Rita (1985), "Military-related Debt in Non-oil Developing Countries," *SIPRI Yearbook 1985*.
Viner, Jacob (1947), "International Finance in the Postwar World," *The Journal of Political Economy* 55, (April).
Wallich, Henry C. (1943), "The Future of Latin American Dollar Bonds," *American Economic Review* 33.
Watkins, Alfred J. (1986), *Till Death Do Us Part: Who Wins, Who Loses, and Who Pays for the International Debt Crisis*, Washington, Roosevelt Center for American Policy Studies.
Weiner, Benjamin (1983), "When We Forgave (or Forgot) Our Debtors," *Wall Street Journal*, November 6.
Wellons, Philip (1977), *Borrowing bvy Developing Countries on the Eurocurrency Market*. Paris: Development Centre of the OECD.
——— (1987), "Bank and the Export Credit Wars: Mixed Credits in the Sicartsa Financing," in *The Export-Import Bank at Fifty*, ed. Rita M. Rodriguez. Lexington Books.
Williams, R.C. et al (1981), *International Capital Markets 1981*, I.M.F. Occasional Paper no.7. Washington International Monetary Fund.
Witcher, S. Karene (1984), "Should Debtors Repudiate? Some feel it would hurt less than current austerity," *Wall Street Journal*, June 22.
World Bank (1982), *Economic Situation and Prospects of India*, Report No.3872–IN.

PERIODICALS

Banking
Business Latin America
Business Week
Euromoney
Finance and Development
Financial Times

Fortune
IMF Survey
International Currency Review
International Herald Tribune
International Monetary Fund, *Annual Report*
New York Times
Wall Street Journal.
World Financial Markets (Morgan Guaranty Trust)
World Bank, *Annual Report*
World Bank, *World Debt Tables*.

Index